Social Studies

myWorld

ACTIVITY GUIDE

3

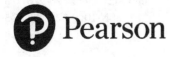 **Pearson**

Boston, Massachusetts   Chandler, Arizona
Glenview, Illinois   New York, New York

Credits appear on page 159, which constitutes an extension of this copyright page.

ISBN-13: 978-0-328-97316-3
ISBN-10: 0-328-97316-5

6 19

Contents

Graphic Organizers

myWorld Activity Guide

How to Use This Book

The *myWorld Activity Guide* was designed for teachers who love social studies but want to teach it in a different way. The program focuses on key topics in social studies, aligning to content frequently taught in each grade from kindergarten to Grade 5. The chapters in this book introduce students to social studies through fun activities and engaging inquiries. You can use the Activity Guide on its own, with associated support materials, or in connection with your basal program.

Teacher Planner

The Chapter Planner outlines the chapter's content in a clear chart with this information:

- **Description** gives a quick overview of each activity and its steps
- **Duration** offers a time estimate, making it easy to plan
- **Materials** lists the materials you will need for each part of the lesson
- **Participants** suggests whether to complete each part of the activity as whole class, small group, or individual

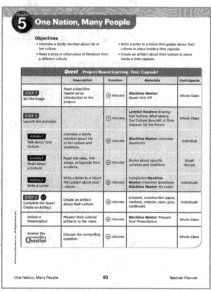

Quest

Each chapter includes detailed lesson suggestions for a long-term inquiry, or Quest.

- Each Quest starts with a Compelling Question, designed to engage students in the inquiry.
- The Quest is set up with three steps: Set the Stage, Launch the Activities, and Complete the Quest.
- Within each step, you'll find suggestions for guiding students to complete a series of activities, culminating in a final product, such as a hands-on project, presentation, civic discussion, or writing project.
- Each chapter contains suggestions for modifying the activities for English Learners.
- Where appropriate, student worksheets are provided to support student completion of the Quest.
- Rubrics in the front of the book will help you and your students evaluate their work.

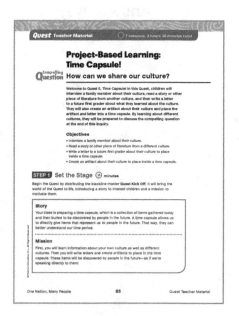

Quick Activities

Each chapter includes detailed lesson suggestions for a series of short activities related to the chapter content. Where appropriate, student worksheets are provided to support student completion of activities. Rubrics in the front of this book will help you and your students evaluate their work on each activity. The Activity Guide also offers suggestions for modifying the activities for English Learners.

Examples of Quick Activities are:

Games	Preparing and Acting Out a Skit
Debates	Building a Social Media Profile
Art Projects	Map Activities

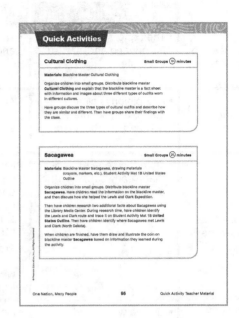

Read Aloud or Readers Theater

Each chapter has a Read Aloud or Readers Theater related to chapter content. With grade-appropriate language, the stories and Readers Theaters bring to life important content related to the chapter.

Graphic Organizers

You will find a wide variety of graphic organizers at the back of this book. You will find many uses for them as your students complete the activities and Quests described in this book.

How to Use This Book

Opinion Writing

Directions: Copy the rubric for individuals or groups (for collaborative writing projects). Rank individuals or groups for each skill.

	4 Excellent	3 Good	2 Satisfactory	1 Needs Improvement
Introduce the topic or text.	• The topic is clearly introduced and is accurate.	• The topic is introduced and is mostly accurate.	• An attempt is made to introduce the topic, but it is incorrect and/or unclear.	• The topic is not introduced.
State an opinion.	• An opinion is clearly stated and accurately responds to the topic.	• An opinion that mostly responds to the topic is stated but is vague.	• An attempt is made to state an opinion, but it does not respond to the topic and/or is unclear.	• An opinion is not stated.
Provide reasons that support the opinion.	• More than one reason that clearly supports the opinion is provided. • All provided reasons are supported with facts and details. (Grades 4–5)	• Only one reason is provided or more than one reason is provided, but the reasons mostly support the opinion. (Grade 3) • Provided reasons are mostly supported with facts and details. (Grades 4–5)	• An attempt is made to provide a reason, but the reason is either unclear or does not support the opinion. (Grade 3) • Facts and details do not clearly support the provided reasons. (Grades 4–5)	• No reasons are provided. (Grade 3) • Provided reasons are not supported with facts or details. (Grades 4–5)
Use linking words and phrases to connect opinion and reasons.	• Linking words and phrases consistently are used correctly to connect the opinion and reasons.	• Linking words and phrases are generally used correctly to connect the opinion and reasons.	• Linking words and phrases are used incorrectly to connect the opinion and reasons.	• Linking words and phrases are not used to connect the opinion and reasons.
Provide a concluding statement or section.	• A concluding statement or section is provided and includes a clear restatement of the opinion without introducing new ideas. (Grade 3) • A concluding statement or section is provided that clearly relates to the opinion without introducing new ideas. (Grades 4–5)	• A concluding statement or section is provided, but it includes a vague restatement of the opinion or introduces new ideas. (Grade 3) • A concluding statement or section is provided that generally relates to the opinion or introduces new ideas. (Grades 4–5)	• An attempt is made to provide a concluding statement or section, but it includes a vague restatement of the opinion and new ideas. (Grade 3) • A concluding statement or section is provided that vaguely relates to the opinion and introduces new ideas. (Grades 4–5)	• A concluding statement or section is not provided.

Informative/Explanatory Writing

Directions: Copy the rubric for individuals or groups (for collaborative writing projects). Rank individuals or groups for each skill.

	4 Excellent	3 Good	2 Satisfactory	1 Needs Improvement
Introduce a topic.	• The topic is clearly introduced and is accurate.	• The topic is introduced and is mostly accurate.	• An attempt is made to introduce the topic but is incorrect and/or unclear.	• The topic is not introduced.
Group related information together.	• Related information is clearly and consistently grouped together.	• Related information is mostly grouped together.	• Related information is sometimes grouped together, but organization of other information is unclear.	• Related information is not grouped together.
Develop the topic with facts, definitions, and details.	• Consistently provides facts, definitions, and details to develop the topic.	• Generally provides facts, definitions, and details to develop the topic.	• Gives some facts, definitions, and details, but they are inaccurate or have a vague link to the topic.	• No information, facts, or definitions are provided.
Use linking words and phrases to connect ideas within categories of information.	• Linking words and phrases consistently are used correctly to connect ideas within categories of information.	• Linking words and phrases are generally used correctly to connect ideas within categories of information.	• Linking words and phrases are used incorrectly to connect ideas within categories of information.	• Linking words and phrases are not used to connect ideas within categories of information.
Provide a concluding statement or section.	• A concluding statement or section is provided and includes a clear restatement of the topic without introducing new ideas. (Grade 3) • A concluding statement or section is provided that clearly relates to the information or explanation presented without introducing new ideas. (Grades 4–5)	• A concluding statement or section is provided, but it includes a vague restatement of the topic or introduces new ideas. (Grade 3) • A concluding statement or section is provided that generally relates to the information or explanation presented or introduces new ideas. (Grades 4–5)	• An attempt is made to provide a concluding statement or section, but it includes a vague restatement of the topic and new ideas. (Grade 3) • A concluding statement or section is provided that vaguely relates to the information or explanation presented and introduces new ideas. (Grades 4–5)	• A concluding statement or section is not provided.

Narrative Writing

Directions: Copy the rubric for individuals or groups (for collaborative writing projects). Rank individuals or groups for each skill.

	4 Excellent	**3** Good	**2** Satisfactory	**1** Needs Improvement
Establish a situation and introduce a narrator and/or characters.	• The situation and the narrator and/or characters are clearly established.	• The situation and the narrator and/or characters are somewhat established.	• The situation and the narrator and/or characters are established but are vague.	• The situation and the narrator and/or characters are not established.
Organize an event sequence that unfolds naturally.	• The event sequence is organized so that it unfolds naturally.	• The event sequence is mostly organized so that it unfolds naturally.	• The event sequence is somewhat organized, but the events unfold awkwardly.	• The event sequence is not organized.
Use dialogue and descriptions to develop experiences and events.	• Dialogue and descriptions are used to clearly and effectively develop experiences and events.	• Some dialogue and descriptions are used to develop experiences and events.	• Dialogue and descriptions are used to develop experiences and events but are vague.	• No dialogue and descriptions are used to develop experiences and events.
Use temporal words and phrases to signal event order. (Grade 3)	• Temporal words and phrases are used consistently and accurately to signal event order.	• Temporal words and phrases are sometimes used to accurately signal event order.	• Temporal words and phrases are occasionally used to signal event order and/or are used inaccurately.	• Temporal words and phrases are not used.
Use a variety of transitional words and phrases to manage the sequence of events. (Grades 4–5)	• A variety of transitional words and phrases are used consistently and accurately to manage the sequence of events.	• A variety of transitional words and phrases are sometimes used to accurately manage the sequence of events.	• Transitional words and phrases are occasionally used to manage the sequence of events and may be used inaccurately or repetitively.	• Transitional words and phrases are not used to manage the sequence of events.
Use concrete words and phrases and sensory details to convey experiences and events. (Grades 4–5)	• Concrete words and phrases and sensory details are used consistently and accurately to convey experiences and events.	• Concrete words and phrases and sensory details are sometimes used to accurately convey experiences and events.	• Concrete words and phrases and sensory details are occasionally used to convey experiences and events and may be used inaccurately or repetitively.	• Concrete words and phrases and sensory details are not used to convey experiences and events.
Provide a sense of closure. (Grade 3)	• A strong sense of closure is provided with a clear ending.	• A sense of closure is provided with a vague ending.	• An attempt is made to provide closure with an ending that trails off.	• A sense of closure is not provided.
Provide a conclusion that follows from the narrated experiences or events. (Grades 4–5)	• A conclusion that clearly follows from the narrated experiences or events is provided.	• A conclusion that mostly follows from the narrated experiences or events is provided.	• A conclusion that loosely follows from the narrated experiences or events is provided.	• A conclusion that follows from the narrated experiences or events is not provided.

Project-Based Learning

Directions: Copy the rubric for individuals or groups. Rank individuals or groups for each skill as they conduct research to complete an inquiry project.

	4 Excellent	3 Good	2 Satisfactory	1 Needs Improvement
PLAN THE INQUIRY: Collaborate to develop a project plan.	• Assigns and accepts tasks within the group, encouraging all group members to play a role and contribute equally. • Engages effectively in collaborative discussions about the inquiry for the duration of the project by explicitly building on others' ideas and expressing their own clearly. • Participates fully in identifying details of the final outcome.	• Accepts tasks within the group, generally encouraging group members to play a role and contribute equally. • Engages in collaborative discussions about the inquiry by building on others' ideas and expressing their own. • Participates in identifying the details for the final outcome.	• Sometimes accepts tasks within the group, occasionally encouraging group members to play a role and contribute equally. • Sometimes engages in collaborative discussions about the inquiry by attempting to build on others' ideas and mostly expressing their own. • Participates somewhat in identifying the details for the final outcome.	• Rarely accepts tasks within the group or encourages group members to play a role and contribute equally. • Rarely engages in collaborative discussions about the inquiry, does not build on others' ideas, and rarely expresses their own. • Does not participate in identifying the details for the final outcome.
DO YOUR RESEARCH: Find sources to support your inquiry.	• Finds relevant evidence in support of own interpretations. • Routinely asks and answers questions, referring to the text to clarify meaning. • Reads or explores a number of sources to gain, modify, or extend knowledge or to learn different perspectives. • Always synthesizes and draws conclusions from information acquired through research.	• Generally finds relevant evidence in support of own interpretations. • Usually asks and answers questions, referring to the text to clarify meaning. • Reads or explores at least one source to gain, modify, or extend knowledge or to learn different perspectives. • Generally synthesizes and draws conclusions from information acquired through research.	• Finds some evidence in support of own interpretations, but some may be irrelevant. • Occasionally asks and answers questions, referring to the text to clarify meaning. • Attempts to read or explore sources but struggles to gain, modify, or extend knowledge. • Attempts to synthesize and draw conclusions from information acquired through research, but conclusions are vague or inaccurate.	• Finds little or no evidence in support of own interpretations. • Rarely or never asks and answers questions or refers to the text to clarify meaning. • Does not attempt to read or explore sources to gain, modify, or extend knowledge. • Does not synthesize or draw conclusions from information acquired through research.
PRODUCE THE PRODUCT: Demonstrate understanding of key ideas.	• Expresses and refines understanding of new concepts while creating the product. • Consistently uses language acquired from research in speaking and writing about the product. • Adds multiple visuals or multimedia components to enhance the product.	• Generally expresses and refines understanding of new concepts while creating the product. • Generally uses language acquired from research in speaking and writing about the product. • Adds at least one visual or multimedia to enhance the product.	• Occasionally expresses and refines understanding of new concepts while creating the product. • Occasionally uses language acquired from research in speaking and writing about the product. • Adds a visual or multimedia, but it is irrelevant and does not enhance the product.	• Rarely expresses and refines understanding of new concepts while creating the product. • Rarely uses language acquired from research in speaking and writing about the product. • Does not include a visual or multimedia.
REFLECT ON THE INQUIRY: Discuss the Compelling Question.	• Fully articulates a meaningful response to the Compelling Question.	• Generally articulates a meaningful response to the Compelling Question.	• Attempts to articulate a response to the Compelling Question, but the response is vague or irrelevant.	• Does not attempt to respond to the Compelling Question.

Collaborative Discussion

Directions: Copy the rubric for individuals, pairs, or groups as they engage in collaborative discussions with diverse partners about grade-appropriate topics and texts, including discussions about current local, national, and international issues. Rank individuals or groups for each skill.

	4 Excellent	3 Good	2 Satisfactory	1 Needs Improvement
Come to discussions prepared.	• Reads/studies all discussion materials prior to discussion. • Explicitly uses information and advance preparation to explore ideas during discussion.	• Reads/studies most discussion materials prior to discussion. • Mostly uses information and advance preparation to explore ideas during discussion.	• Reads/studies some discussion materials prior to discussion. • Occasionally uses information and advanced preparation to explore ideas during discussion.	• Reads/studies little if any discussion materials prior to discussion. • Does not use information and advanced preparation to explore ideas during discussion.
Follow agreed-upon rules for discussions.	• Follows agreed-upon rules at all times. • Carries out all assigned roles. (G4–5) • Consistently uses deliberative processes when making group decisions.	• Follows agreed-upon rules most of the time. • Carries out most assigned roles. (G4–5) • Generally uses deliberative processes when making group decisions.	• Follows agreed-upon rules but needs occasional direction. • Carries out some assigned roles with direction and reminders. (G4–5) • Sometimes uses deliberative processes when making group decisions.	• Does not follow agreed-upon rules without teacher direction. • Does not carry out assigned roles. (G4–5) • Does not use deliberative processes when making group decisions.
Pose and respond to specific questions to clarify or follow up on information.	• Uses questions and responses that explicitly clarify or follow up on the information presented and purposefully contributes to the discussion. • Poses questions that clearly link to the remarks of others.	• Uses questions and responses that generally clarify or follow up on the information presented and contributes to the discussion. • Poses questions that mostly link to the remarks of others.	• Attempts to use questions and responses that clarify or follow up on the information presented and attempts to contribute to the discussion. • Poses questions that vaguely link to the remarks of others.	• Does not use questions or responses that clarify or follow up on the information presented and does not contribute to the discussion. • Does not pose questions that link to the remarks of others.
Report on a topic.	• Thoroughly explains ideas and understanding in light of the discussion. • Expresses key ideas clearly. (G4–5) • Always provides facts that are appropriate to the discussion and details that are descriptive and relevant. • Always speaks clearly at an understandable pace. • Consistently raises reasons and evidence supporting particular points. (G4–5)	• Mostly explains ideas and understanding in light of the discussion. • Generally expresses key ideas clearly. (G4–5) • Usually provides facts that are appropriate to the discussion and details that are descriptive and relevant. • Generally speaks clearly at an understandable pace. • Mostly raises reasons and evidence supporting particular points. (G4–5)	• Attempts to explain ideas and understanding in light of the discussion. • Occasionally expresses key ideas, but they may not be clear. (G4–5) • Provides facts and details, but some facts and details may not be descriptive or relevant. • Attempts to speak clearly at an understandable pace but is difficult to understand at times. • Occasionally raises reasons and evidence, but these do not always support particular points. (G4–5)	• Rarely explains ideas and understanding in light of the discussion. • Rarely if ever expresses key ideas. (G4–5) • Does not provide facts or details. • Does not speak clearly or at an understandable pace. • Rarely if ever raises reasons and evidence supporting particular points. (G4–5)

Readers Theater/Read Aloud

Directions: Copy the rubric for individuals or groups. Rank individuals or groups for each skill.

	4 Excellent	3 Good	2 Satisfactory	1 Needs Improvement
BEFORE READING: Research and practice part.	• Plans own part and practices reading aloud with correct projection and diction. • Consistently uses context to confirm or self-correct word recognition and understanding, rereading as necessary. • Consistently applies grade-level phonics and word analysis skills in decoding words.	• Plans part with some assistance and practices reading aloud with mostly correct projection and diction. • Usually uses context to confirm or self-correct word recognition and understanding. • Usually applies grade-level phonics and word analysis skills in decoding words.	• Attempts to plan own part and practices reading aloud with sometimes incorrect projection and diction. • Occasionally uses context to confirm or self-correct word recognition and understanding. • Sometimes applies grade-level phonics and word analysis skills in decoding words.	• Does not plan own part or practice reading aloud. • Rarely if ever uses context to confirm or self-correct word recognition or understanding. • Rarely if ever applies grade-level phonics and word analysis skills in decoding words.
WHILE READING ALOUD OR PERFORMING: Communicate meaning with clear use of language and enthusiastic delivery.	• Consistently reads text with clear purpose and understanding, speaking clearly at an understandable pace. • Consistently reads prose orally with accuracy, appropriate rate, and expression on successive readings to support comprehension. • Understands the movement in front of a group; consistently maintains appropriate eye contact.	• Generally reads text with clear purpose and understanding, usually speaking clearly at an understandable pace. • Generally reads prose orally with accuracy, appropriate rate, and expression on successive readings to support comprehension. • Usually understands the movement in front of a group; usually maintains appropriate eye contact.	• Attempts to read text with purpose and understanding but sometimes does not speak clearly or at an understandable pace. • Reads prose orally but there are a few errors in accuracy, rate, and/or expression, even on successive readings. • Sometimes understands the movement in front of a group; attempts to maintain appropriate eye contact.	• Does not read text with clear purpose or understanding. • Does not read prose orally with accuracy, appropriate rate, or expression, even on successive readings. • Does not understand the movement in front of a group or maintain eye contact.
AFTER READING: Ask and answer questions about a reading of a text.	• Consistently asks clear questions related to the topic to check their own understanding of information presented. • Always links comments to the remarks of others. • Consistently offers appropriate elaboration and details.	• Often asks questions related to the topic to check their own understanding of information presented. • Often links comments to the remarks of others. • Often offers appropriate elaboration and details.	• Occasionally asks questions related to the topic to check their own understanding of information presented. • Occasionally links comments to the remarks of others. • Occasionally offers elaboration and details but may not be appropriate to the topic.	• Rarely if ever asks questions related to the topic to check their own understanding of information presented. • Rarely if ever links comments to the remarks of others. • Rarely if ever offers elaboration and details.
AFTER READING: Demonstrate comprehension of text.	• Accurately determines the main ideas and supporting details of a text read aloud. • Clearly distinguishes between own point of view and that of the narrator or characters.	• Usually determines the main ideas and supporting details of a text read aloud accurately. • Generally distinguishes between own point of view and that of the narrator or characters.	• Sometimes determines the main ideas and supporting details of a text read aloud but is not always accurate. • Has difficulty with distinguishing between own point of view and that of the narrator or characters.	• Rarely if ever determines the main ideas and supporting details of a text read aloud. • Is unable to distinguish between own point of view and that of the narrator or characters.

Objectives

- Identify and describe physical features, such as landforms and bodies of water, of different regions of the United States.
- Describe the weather and climate in different regions.

- Identify resources in each region of the United States.
- Create and use maps to explain the physical geography of each region of the United States.

Quest   Project-Based Learning: Mapping One Hundred Miles

	Description	Duration	Materials	Participants
STEP 1 Set the Stage	Read a blackline master as an introduction to the project.	15 minutes	**Blackline Master:** Quest Kick Off	Whole Class
STEP 2 Launch the Activities	Watch a video with background information.	5 minutes	**Video:** Discover the World of Nature	Whole Class
Activity 1 Mapping U.S. Regions	Make a salt dough map of the five regions of the United States.	45 minutes	**Student Activity Mats:** 1A United States, Physical; 2B United States Outline; flour, salt, water, cream of tartar, 8-by-10 piece of cardboard, paint	Individuals
Activity 2 Greetings From…	Design a postcard from one of the five regions of the United States.	30 minutes	**Blackline Master:** The Five Regions of the United States, index cards, crayons, sample postcards	Individuals
Activity 3 Regional Weather Collage	Make a weather collage of a region.	30 minutes	old magazines, poster board, glue, markers	Small Groups
Activity 4 Mapping the Race Course	Develop a 100-mile course map.	45 minutes	**Student Activity Mat:** 1A United States, Physical; poster board, rulers, markers	Small Groups
STEP 3 ELL Complete the Quest Prepare a Presentation	Prepare a presentation describing the features of the race-course map.	30 minutes	completed maps	Small Groups
Deliver a Presentation	Deliver a presentation to the producers of *One Hundred Miles.*	45 minutes		Small Groups
Answer the **Compelling Question**	How do physical features affect us?	15 minutes		Whole Class

Quick Activities

	Description	Duration	Materials	Participants
Ecosystem Mobile	Make a mobile of one U.S. ecosystem.	(30) minutes	string, glue, markers, coat hangers, pictures of ecosystems	Small Groups
Protecting Resources: Design a Book Jacket	Design a book jacket and a summary for a book about the use of local resources.	(30) minutes	**Leveled Readers:** *Let's Protect the Planet; Saving the Planet;* and *Protecting the Planet;* **Content Reader:** *The 10 Greatest Threats to Earth*	Individuals
Start a Web Site or Video Channel	Describe an agricultural or industrial region of the United States.	(30) minutes	**Blackline Master:** Start a Web Site or Video Channel, computers, paper, markers	Individuals
Regions Game	Play a game about the five regions of the United States.	(15) minutes	**Blackline Master:** The Five Regions of the United States	Whole Class
Readers Theater: Train Trip	Stage a reading of a script about a family's train trip across the United States.	(30) minutes	**Blackline Master:** Train Trip	Whole Class

Project-Based Learning: Mapping One Hundred Miles

Compelling Question How do physical features affect us?

Welcome to Quest 1, Mapping One Hundred Miles. In this Quest, your students will create and present an annotated map of a region of the United States. By mapping an area, they will gain hands-on insight to help answer the compelling question at the end of this inquiry.

Objectives

- Identify and describe physical features, such as landforms and bodies of water, of different regions of the United States.
- Describe the weather and climate in different regions.
- Identify resources in each region of the United States.
- Create and use maps to explain the physical geography of each region of the United States.

STEP 1 Set the Stage ⏱ 15 minutes

Begin the Quest by distributing the blackline master **Quest Kick Off.** It will bring the world of the Quest to life, introducing a story to interest students and a mission to motivate them.

Story

The reality TV show *One Hundred Miles* wants to film new episodes. Each week on the show, three contestants set out on a 100-mile journey through the wilderness. Each contestant tries to finish the 100-mile course first. The producers of the show are looking for good routes to film for the next season.

Mission

Students must pick a region of the United States in which to develop a race course. It should have some geographical challenges, such as a river to cross, steep climbs, or other challenges. Their mission is to work in groups to prepare a map of a race course to present to the show's producers.

STEP 2 Launch the Activities

The following four activities will help students research and develop an annotated course map. Note that all four can be done independently of the larger Quest.

Begin by showing the video Discover the World of Nature, which will give students information about the environment that they will need to complete the activities. You may also assign the appropriate Leveled Reader for this chapter.

Then organize students into small groups that will remain consistent for all the activities.

Activity 1   Mapping U.S. Regions    45 minutes

Materials: Student Activity Mats: 1A United States, Physical; 2B United States Outline; flour, salt, water, cream of tartar, 8-by-10 piece of cardboard, paint

Distribute Student Activity Mats 1A United States, Physical and 2B United States Outline. Students use these mats to help them make a 3-D map of the physical features of the United States using salt dough.

Instruct students to paste the outline map of the United States on cardboard.

Next have each student create salt dough by mixing together 4 cups of flour, 2 cups of salt, 2 cups of water, and 2 tablespoons of cream of tartar. Instruct students to press the dough onto the map until the entire outline has been filled. Guide students to model the features by pinching the dough together for mountains or pressing the dough apart to create valleys and waterways. Have students refer to the physical map to help them create landforms in the correct places.

Finally, have students paint the dough after it has dried: blue for water, green for coastal plains, yellow for the Great Plains, and brown for mountains. Have students draw a map legend and add labels onto the cardboard for the five regions of the United States: the West region, the Midwest region, the Northeast region, the Southwest region, and the Southeast region. Students may wish to shade national borders and label oceans.

Due to time constraints, 3-D relief maps can replace the salt dough project (for example, use modeling clay to represent the features).

Materials: Blackline Master: The Five Regions of the United States,
index cards, crayons, sample postcards

Provide students with the blackline master **The Five Regions of the United States,**
which lists facts about the five regions. Read through the facts with students, and
as a class identify each region. Explain to students that they will make postcards
from one of the regions of the United States.

Show sample postcards. Group students into five regional groups (Northeast,
Southeast, Midwest, Southwest, West). There should be at least one group for
each region. Note that students will stay in these groups for the remainder of the
Quest.

Instruct groups to examine landforms, recreational activities, and interesting facts
about their region. Provide groups with books and resources.

Distribute a large index card to each student. Instruct students to create a
postcard from their region. Have students draw a picture on one side, and write
a descriptive paragraph to a friend on the other side. The paragraph should
describe two recreational activities from that region. Have students draw a stamp,
and address the postcard as if they were mailing it.

Activity 3 Regional Weather Collage ⏱30 minutes

Materials: Magazines for cutting out pictures of physical features, poster board, glue, markers

In their regional groups, have students make a collage of images that show the climate of their region. Ask students to locate images of weather and the effects of the climate on people in the region.

Provide resources to each group, such as photos of the landscape, and photos of resources (plants and animals) in the regions. Students can draw illustrations, too, if they prefer.

Distribute poster board to each group so that students can paste their images to make a regional weather collage. Finally, have students write an informative paragraph describing the climate of their region. Remind students to include a topic sentence, at least three sentences with details, and a concluding sentence.

You may want to have students visit the following Web sites:

https://www.ready.gov. Use the search words "Kids" and "Know the Facts, Be Empowered!"
https://www.fema.gov. Use the search words "Disaster Fact Sheets for Kids."
https://water.usgs.gov. Use the search words "Water Science School" and "water surface information."
https://gis.ncdc.noaa.gov/

Activity 4 Mapping the Race Course ⏱45 minutes

Materials: Student Activity Mat: 1A United States, Physical; poster board, rulers, markers

Draw a Map
Have groups choose at least three natural elements to include in their race course map (for example, a river, a mountain, and wild animals). Then have students draw their course map onto poster board.

Remind students to add a starting point and finish line that covers 100 miles. Instruct students to include five markers or pop-up points on the course. These should contain four physical features from the region (rivers, lakes, mountains, valleys, deserts, forest, cliffs, hills/inclines) and at least two supporting pictures.

Make sure students also include at least one challenge marker on the map that tells about potential weather, animal, or physical hazards in the area (for example, beware of rattlesnakes, bear crossing, rock slides, avalanches, tornado alley, hurricane zone, tsunami area, snow gear needed, excessive heat, last water for 50 miles, and so on). Remind students that the course map should be challenging and entertaining for the viewing audience. The map should not be a straight line, and it does not have to follow established roads or trails.

Part 1 Prepare a Presentation (30) minutes

Materials: completed maps

After students have completed the activities, including the annotated course map, have them work in teams to prepare and deliver their race course idea to the reality show producers. Suggest that students divide their race course into sections to be presented by each person.

Remind students about the Quest mission. Students should present as if they are talking to producers of the show *One Hundred Miles* to convince them to use their course. How can they convince them that their course is challenging and entertaining?

Use the Project-Based Learning rubric to assess the project.

ELL Support for English Language Learners

Writing Have students construct precise and detailed sentences that connect ideas to describe their geographic region.

Entering: Encourage students to draw a picture of one landform, plant, animal, or weather in their region. Help students label their drawing.

Emerging: Ask students to write and illustrate two short facts about their region. Then invite pairs to take turns sharing and stating their facts. Help students write the compound sentence using *and, but,* or *so*. (For example, It's green. It's prickly. Combined: It's green and prickly.)

Developing: Ask students to write two short facts about their region. Then invite them to work together to write the two facts in one sentence. Help students use *and, but,* or *so* to connect the two facts into one sentence. (For example, It is cold there. It is snowy. Combined: It is cold and snowy there.)

Expanding: Ask students to write three facts about their region. Have pairs work together to state these three facts in a sentence or two. (For example, The region has a desert. The desert has cactuses. The cactuses have thorns. Combined: The region has a desert with thorny cactuses.)

Bridging: Ask students to list facts about their region. Then have students write these facts in a paragraph that flows logically from one idea to the next. Have pairs share their paragraphs and work together to revise and improve the paragraphs.

Part 2 Deliver a Presentation 45 minutes

Simulate a real-life panel of *One Hundred Mile* producers (made up of classmates, parents, or community members).

Before students present, have them divide up the course, so each member has a turn to speak. Allow time for each student to make notes of the main points they want to cover. Have each student mark the places on their map that they want to talk about.

Then have each group present and sell their race course. Encourage students to speak slowly, clearly, and in a loud voice. When they finish speaking, remind them to ask the audience members if they have any questions.

Part 3 Answer the Compelling Question 15 minutes

After students present their race course ideas, encourage them to reflect on what they learned. As a class, discuss the compelling question for this Quest "How do physical features affect us?"

Students have learned about the five main regions of the United States, including the location, physical features, climate, recreational activities, and natural resources of each. Encourage students to think about how these features affect people. Students should use what they learned to answer the compelling question.

Mapping One Hundred Miles

The reality TV show *One Hundred Miles* wants to film new episodes for next season. On the show, three contestants race to finish a 100-mile journey through the wilderness. The first person to finish wins.

The show's producers need more race courses to film for next season. They need your help to find new courses.

Your Mission

The makers of the reality TV show *One Hundred Miles* have chosen your team to present a 100-mile race course map for an episode next season. They need a challenging and interesting course in one of the five regions of the United States.

To make and present your 100-mile race course map, work with your team to do the following:

Activity 1 **Mapping U.S. Regions:** Make a salt dough map of the United States.

Activity 2 **Greetings From . . . :** Design and write a postcard.

Activity 3 **Regional Weather Collage:** Collect and assemble weather images.

Activity 4 **Mapping the Race Course:** Make a map of your 100-mile race course.

Complete Your Quest

Present your 100-mile race course map to the show's producers.

Name _____ Date _____

The Five Regions of the United States

Answer the questions to analyze the five regions of the United States.

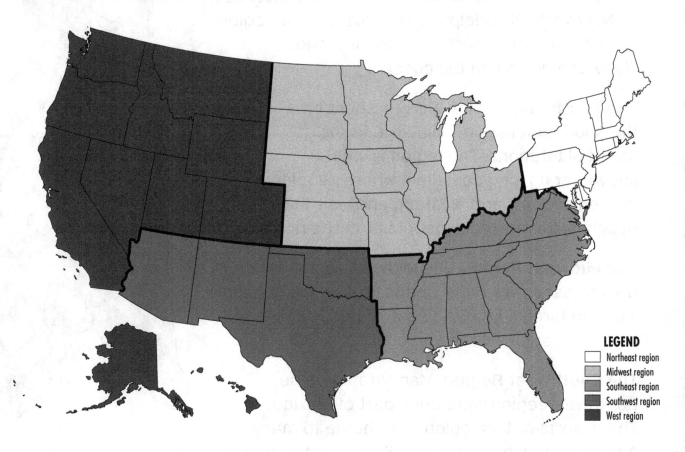

LEGEND
- Northeast region
- Midwest region
- Southeast region
- Southwest region
- West region

1. In which region will you find the Rio Grande River? _____

2. Which is the most southern region in which you will find the Appalachian Mountains? _____

3. What region is south of the Ohio River? _____

4. Which region has the fewest states? _____

5. Which region has the smallest states? _____

6. In what regions will you find the Mississippi River? _____

7. In which region will you find Alaska? _____

Facts About the Five Regions

The Northeast Region The Northeast region has some of the largest cities in the United States, such as New York, Philadelphia, and Boston. The region has hills, a rocky coastline, and farmland. Many people fish on the coast.

The Southeast Region Early settlers in the Southeast region built large farms called plantations. The region is well known for its long coastline, where people fish, enjoy the warm weather, and visit the beaches. Inland, many people farm the rich soil.

The Midwest Region The Midwest region is one of the flattest areas in the United States. Many people work on farms in the Midwest. Other people mine materials, such as iron and coal.

The Southwest Region Many states in the Southwest region were once part of Mexico. The deserts of this region were home to many American Indian groups. The Southwest region is hot and dry. It has many landforms including plains, deserts, mountains, and canyons. Its most famous canyon is the Grand Canyon.

The West Region The West region has many mountains. The Rocky Mountains have some of the tallest mountains in the United States. Other mountain ranges include the Coast Range and the Alaska Range. The West also has a long coastline. There people fish, hike, camp, and visit the beaches. Some of the West is forested; other parts are farmed.

Quick Activities

Ecosystem Mobile

Small Groups minutes

Materials: string, glue, markers, coat hangers, pictures of ecosystems

Provide books about U.S. ecosystems to the class. Make sure to include information about the following ecosystems: deserts, grasslands, woodlands, forested mountains, coastal forests, wetlands, lakes, and beaches.

Have students select one of the ecosystems in the United States. Then invite them to make an ecosystem mobile, which includes resources, goods, and services the ecosystem provides, as well as pictures of how people use these resources.

Put students into ecosystem groups. Students in each group will create a mobile as follows:

- First string: Name and description of ecosystem
- Second string: Resources the ecosystem provides
- Third string: Pictures of goods and services the ecosystem provides
- Fourth string: Pictures of humans in the ecosystem using its resources with an explanatory sentence

Protecting Resources: Design a Book Jacket

Individuals  minutes

Materials: Leveled Readers: *Let's Protect the Planet; Saving the Planet;* and *Protecting the Planet;* Content Reader: *The 10 Greatest Threats to Earth*

Students design a book jacket for a book they plan to write about the use of local resources. Read aloud the book *One Plastic Bag: Isatou Ceesay and the Recycling Women of the Gambia* by Miranda Paul, *A River Ran Wild* by Lynne Cherry, or a similar book. Discuss how small actions can make a big difference, and how people have used local resources to change their environment.

Encourage students to think of a story they could tell that takes place in your local environment. Tell students they will design a book jacket for their story. Instruct students to develop a title, draw a front cover illustration, and write a back cover summary.

Start a Web Site or Video Channel

Individuals (30) minutes

Materials: Blackline Master: Start a Web Site or Video Channel, computers, paper, markers

Invite students to make a Web site or start a video channel about an agricultural or industrial region of the United States.

Distribute the blackline master **Start a Web Site or Video Channel** and point out the agricultural and industrial regions. Help students identify the industrial products in each region.

Show students existing Web sites about these types of regions and discuss the elements and purpose of a Web page. This Web site can provide examples and data: https://www.nationalgeographic.org. Use the search words "North America Resources." The Bureau of Labor Statistics site, https://www.bls.gov has information that you can supply to your students. Use the search words "Industries at a Glance."

Instruct students to include the following:

- At least three facts about the agricultural or industrial region
- Location of the region (including a map)
- Photos of the agriculture or industry
- An opinion about the agriculture or industry

....

ELL Support for English Language Learners

Speaking Have students describe their region to a partner.

Entering: Invite students to draw a picture of a plant or animal found on a farm in their region. Beneath the picture help students label the picture. Then have students say aloud the name of the plant or animal to a partner.

Emerging: Invite students to use the following sentence frames to describe the agriculture of their region to a partner: *A plant grown on a farm in my region is ____. A farm animal in my region is ____.*

Developing: Encourage students to describe to a partner agricultural or industrial products found in their region. They can use these sentence starters to help:
An important agricultural/industrial product is . . .
This product is important because . . .

Expanding: Encourage students to describe to a partner agricultural or industrial products found in their region. They should use complete sentences in their descriptions, and tell why the products are important to the region.

Bridging: Have students write a paragraph about agricultural or industrial products found in their region. Then have them present their paragraph to a partner. They should use good transitions between sentences, and give an opinion about the future of the industry in the region.

Regions Game

Materials: Blackline Master: The Five Regions of the United States

Designate five places in the classroom as a specific region (Northeast, Southeast, Midwest, Southwest, and West). Then read aloud to students a fact from the blackline master The Five Regions of the United States. After students hear each fact, have them move to the correct region in the classroom.

Readers Theater: Train Trip

Whole Class 30 minutes

Materials: Blackline Master: Train Trip

Distribute the blackline master **Train Trip** to students. Explain that in the story, a family is planning a trip across the United States. They want to see three features along the route.

Point out elements of a script, including the roles and dialogue. Explain that the director's notes give information about the play that is not included in the dialogue.

Assign roles and have students read aloud the script. Tell students they should try to read with accuracy, at an appropriate speed, and with expression. Remind students that listeners should pay close attention, and be respectful, polite, and interested.

Start a Web Site or Video Channel

Use this map to help you write content for your Web site or video channel.

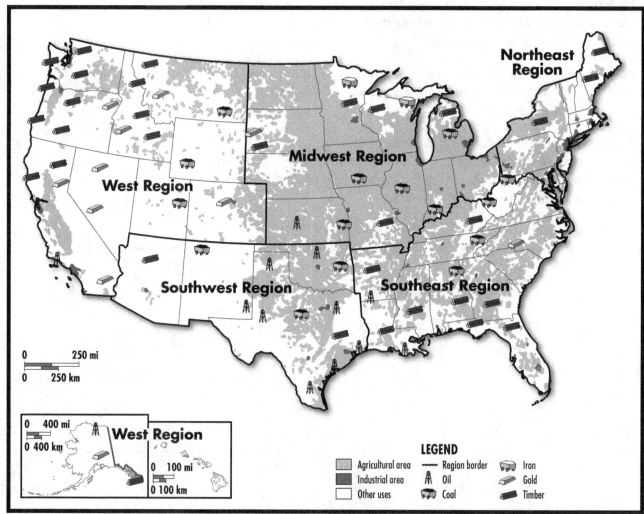

Northeast Region

Midwest Region

West Region

Southwest Region

Southeast Region

0   250 mi

0   250 km

0   400 mi

0   400 km

West Region

0   100 mi

0   100 km

LEGEND

Agricultural area	— Region border	Iron
Industrial area	Oil	Gold
Other uses	Coal	Timber

Readers Theater
Train Trip

A story about a family's summer train trip.

The Parts
- **Mom**
- **Dad**
- **Maria**
- **Todd**
- **Train Conductor**
- **Narrator**

Director's Notes:

The play begins with the family planning a summer trip. They have special train tickets across the United States from San Francisco to New York. The tickets let them make three stops. The play follows the family as they make plans.

Narrator: It's a beautiful summer day. A family of four boards a train. They each have a special ticket, so they have some decisions to make.

Train Conductor: Nice! I see you bought the family summer special tickets. You can get off and on in three places along the route from San Francisco to New York. I'm sure you'll see a lot of fun things on the way!

Mom: You heard the conductor—let's choose three stops. Which ones should we choose?

Dad:
studying a map
Looks like we can get off at Salt Lake City, Utah. Should we go see the Great Salt Lake?

Todd:
looking at photos on travel brochure

Wow! Look at that! The train passes right next to the Great Salt Lake—only feet from the water.

Maria:
looking at guide book

After that, we can go east to Denver. Denver is called the Mile-High City because it is 5,280 feet above sea level.

Todd:

Yeah, I know that! We learned that in school this year. It's the highest major city in the United States.

Mom:
holding up fingers as she lists each stop

Wow, you two have learned a lot about geography this year! So, it sounds like we're stopping in Salt Lake City and Denver. We have one more stop. What should it be?

Dad:

Well, I think we should be adventurous. It's summer vacation after all. How about we get off in the great city of Chicago?

Todd:

Terrific! I've never been so far east before. What should we do in Chicago?

Maria:

It's soooo big! Maybe we can see a musical play. There's a famous one in Chicago right now.

Dad:

Yes, I know. You sing the songs all the time.

Mom:

I'll let the conductor know that we're getting off at Salt Lake City. Then we can explore and board another train to Denver. From there, we'll move on to Chicago. After that, we'll continue to our final destination, New York City!

Objectives
- Discuss the reasons the economy can change.
- Identify and describe the three types of resources: natural resources, human resources, and capital resources.
- Create a presentation about one of our nation's leading industries.

Quest Project-Based Learning: Industries of Tomorrow				
	Description	Duration	Materials	Participants
STEP 1 Set the Stage	Read a blackline master as an introduction to the project.	15 minutes	**Blackline Master:** Quest Kick Off	Small Groups
STEP 2 Launch the Activities	Watch a video with background information.	15 minutes	**Leveled Readers:** How Do Industries Grow?; Technology and California; Silicon Valley **Video:** Farmers Market: Meet Me at Third and Fairfax	Whole Class
Activity 1 Goods and Services	Research to determine the goods and services provided by an industry.	40 minutes	**Graphic Organizer:** T-Chart, classroom or Library Media Center resources	Small Groups
Activity 2 Resources	Research types of resources needed in an industry.	30 minutes	**Student Activity Mat:** 3A Graphic Organizer Classroom or Library Media Center resources	Small Groups
Activity 3 Strengths and Weaknesses	Research strengths and weaknesses of one American industry.	35 minutes	**Blackline Master:** Strengths and Weaknesses	Small Groups
Activity 4 Preparing the Presentation Board	Create a presentation board to accompany the presentation about one of our nation's industries.	40 minutes	Presentation boards **Graphic Organizer:** Four-Column Chart	Small Groups
STEP 3 ELL Complete the Quest Prepare a Presentation	Prepare the presentation and select the industry that will be the strongest in ten years.	30 minutes	**Blackline Master:** The Nation's Strongest Industry	Whole Class
Deliver a Presentation	Deliver a presentation to the class and to other audience members using the presentation boards.	30 minutes		Whole Class
Answer the **Compelling Question**	Reflect on leading industries and discuss the compelling question.	20 minutes		Whole Class

	Quick Activities			
	Description	**Duration**	**Materials**	**Participants**
Industries of the World	Discuss other locations that are top producers of similar items around the world.	25 minutes	**Student Activity Mat:** 5B The World Outline chart paper	Whole Class
Entrepreneur	Create a business model for a new product or service.	30 minutes	**Blackline Master:** Business Model	Individuals
Past and Present ELL	Create a Venn diagram to show how a selected industry has changed from the past to present.	35 minutes	**Graphic Organizer:** Venn Diagram, classroom or Library Media Center resources	Small Groups
Readers Theater: Internet Oranges	Perform a script about a small family planning their business for future generations.	25 minutes	**Blackline Master:** Internet Oranges	Whole Class

Project-Based Learning: Industries of Tomorrow

Q Compelling Question **How does the economy change?**

Welcome to Quest 2, Industries of Tomorrow. Students will explore different industries to gain a basic understanding of the economy of the United States. Students will then prepare a presentation about one of our nation's leading industries. After completing these activities, students will be able to discuss the compelling question at the end of this inquiry.

Objectives

• Discuss the reasons the economy can change.
• Identify and describe the three types of resources: natural resources, human resources, and capital resources.
• Create a presentation about one of our nation's leading industries.

STEP 1   Set the Stage   ⑮ minutes

Begin the Quest by distributing the blackline master **Quest Kick Off.** It will bring the world of the Quest to life, introducing a story to interest students and a mission to motivate them.

Story

The United States Bureau of Economic and Business Affairs is collecting research for a new report. The report will show people how important American industries are. They are asking students to determine which industry will be the strongest in ten years.

....

Mission

In groups, students will select an industry and prepare a report and presentation that explains the types of resources needed, the goods and services the industry provides, and the industry's strengths and weaknesses. Students will conclude their mission by predicting how strong the industry will be in ten years.

STEP 2 Launch the Activities

The following four activities will help students prepare for their presentation about one of America's leading industries. Note that all four can be done independently of the larger Quest.

Begin by showing the chapter video, "Farmers Market: Meet Me at Third and Fairfax," which will show students some aspects of the agriculture, fishing, and manufacturing industries. You may also assign the appropriate leveled reader for this chapter.

Activity 1 — Goods and Services (40) minutes

Materials: Graphic Organizer: T-Chart, classroom or Library Media Center resources

Small groups conduct research to determine the types of goods and services provided by an industry.

Ask students to brainstorm a list of jobs that they know. Explain to students that these jobs are all part of something larger, known as the economy. Define *economy* as the production, distribution, and usage of wealth, goods, and services. If students lack concepts of economics, consider sharing books such as *The History of Money: From Bartering to Banking* by Martin Jenkins to build background.

Explain *goods* as things that can be used for a specific purpose, such as pencils. Explain that a *service* is work people do, such as cutting hair. *Consumers* are the people who pay for goods and services. *Producers* are the companies who provide the goods and services. Our economy is made up of all of these parts.

Explain that the United States has many different industries. These industries can be divided into categories based on the goods and services they provide. Write the following five industries on the board, and divide students into corresponding research groups:

- Agriculture
- Manufacturing and Technology
- Transportation
- Healthcare
- Real Estate

Distribute the graphic organizer T-Chart to students. Have students record information about the goods (Column 1) and services (Column 2) produced in their industry. Have students research their industry, and give them time to record notes.

Finally, ask students to share what goods and services are produced in their industry. Ask, "How does the local region affect which goods and services an industry provides?"

Activity 2 Resources ⏲ 30 minutes

Materials: Classroom or Library Media Center resources, Student Activity Mat 3A Graphic Organizer

Explain that for companies to succeed, they need to have access to three types of resources:

1. Natural Resources: Items found in nature that people use, such as trees, water, and minerals.

2. Human Resources: People's talents and skills (people involved in making or doing something within an industry).

3. Capital Resources: Human-made items used to make goods or provide services, such as barns, machines, trucks, and stores.

Divide students into their research groups. Instruct groups to research the resources needed in their industry. Give them the following prompt to use as a research guide:

What natural, human, and capital resources does your industry use to make or do what it does?

Instruct students to record the information gathered using Student Activity Mat 3A Graphic Organizer. Suggest that they use a search engine to find information on the types of resources used by their industries.

Ask students to think about the natural resources used in their industries. Ask, "How do you think your industry has changed over the past 100 years in the way it gets or uses the natural resources?"

Activity 3 | Strengths and Weaknesses  35 minutes

Materials: Blackline Master: Strengths and Weaknesses

Explain that another important aspect of the economy is understanding the strengths and weaknesses of various industries. A strength is something that has a positive impact on the industry. It adds value and helps the industry make money. Ask students to brainstorm lists of potential strengths of their industries.

Explain that a weakness is something that slows down growth. For example, the cost of natural resources could affect growth. Ask students to identify other examples of weaknesses in their industries.

Distribute the blackline master **Strengths and Weaknesses.** Read through the questions with students, and instruct groups to research more about their selected industries in order to answer the questions.

After students have had time to research, instruct groups to discuss how important their industry is to the economy of the United States. Then ask groups to share their responses with the class.

Activity 4 | Preparing the Presentation Board 40 minutes

Materials: Presentation boards, Graphic Organizer: Four-Column Chart

Tell students that they will be presenting their research about one industry to the class. Distribute presentation boards to groups.

Write the following on the board:

- Explain the industry.

- Describe the types of goods and/or services provided.

- Describe the types of resources needed.

- Describe the strengths and weaknesses.

Inform students that they need to include all of this information on their boards in a visually appealing way. Discuss how to plan the boards and encourage students to include visuals, such as pictures of products, resources, or graphs. Distribute the graphic organizer **Four-Column Chart** for students to use to document the information for the presentation board.

Part 1 **Prepare a Presentation** (30) minutes

Materials: Blackline Master: The Nation's Strongest Industry

Prepare students for their presentations by giving them time to decide how they want to present their findings. Remind groups that they will vote at the end of the presentations on which industry they think will be the strongest ten years from now.

Distribute the blackline master **The Nation's Strongest Industry.** Read the questions at the bottom of the blackline master and discuss how to best support an answer. Make sure students know that they will be selecting an industry based on facts and information from the presentations. Encourage them to think about how the economy can change.

ⒺⓁⓁ Support for English Language Learners

Speaking Review how to prepare for an oral presentation by planning the presentation, practicing what will be said, and supporting opinions or facts with evidence from research.

Entering: Invite students to select one important American industry. Have them draw a picture of something related to that industry. Beneath the picture, have them label and say the industry.

Emerging: Ask students to write the name of an industry and two resources the industry needs to be successful. Give students the following sentence frames to practice delivering a brief oral presentation: _____ *makes* _____. *It needs* _____ *and* _____ *to be successful.* Then have students practice by delivering their presentations to partners.

Developing: Ask students to write the name of an industry. Have them think about two or three resources that industry needs. Then have students complete these sentence starters: *My industry... Resources it uses are... Important facts about my industry are...* Have students practice reading their sentences aloud to a partner.

Expanding: Ask students to write the name of an industry and three to four facts about the types of resources the industry needs. Instruct students to give one fact from their research to support their statements. Give students time to practice explaining which resources are necessary to succeed and why. Then have students practice delivering their presentations to partners, explaining how the resources are essential to their industry's businesses.

Bridging: Ask students to write the name of an industry and three to four facts about the strengths and weaknesses of the industry. Instruct students to give one fact from their research to support their statements. Give students time to practice explaining the strengths and weaknesses. Encourage them to explain how resources are important when considering strengths and weaknesses. Then have students practice delivering their presentations to partners.

Part 2 Deliver a Presentation 🕒 30 minutes

Give groups time to set up their presentation boards in a museum-style exhibit. Then lead the class and other audience members from exhibit to exhibit while groups present their findings about American industries. Once students have presented, collect students' forms and tally the votes for the strongest industry. Share results with students and foster a conversation using the following prompts:

What makes an industry strong? Will the industry we voted upon be the strongest because things are going to change or because things will remain the same? What industry received the least votes? Do you believe that industry is the least likely to succeed because things are going to change or remain the same?

Part 3 Answer the Compelling Question 🕒 20 minutes

Encourage students to reflect on what they learned. As a class, discuss the compelling question for this Quest: "How does the economy change?"

Students have learned and discussed elements of a successful industry. They have identified goods and services produced, resources used and needed, and strengths and weaknesses of various industries. They should use what they learned to answer the compelling question.

Quest Kick Off

Industries of Tomorrow

The United States Bureau of Economic and Business Affairs is collecting research for a new report. The report will show people how important American industries are. They are asking students to help with the report by determining which industry will be the strongest in ten years.

Your Mission

In groups, select an industry and prepare a report. Explain the types of resources needed, the goods and services the industry provides, and its strengths and weaknesses. Then predict how strong you think the industry will be in ten years.

To present about one of America's leading industries, do the following:

Activity 1 **Goods and Services:** Research to determine the types of goods and services provided by an industry.

Activity 2 **Resources:** Research to determine the types of resources needed within an industry.

Activity 3 **Strengths and Weaknesses:** Research strengths and weaknesses of an industry.

Activity 4 **Preparing the Presentation Board:** Create a presentation board about one industry.

Complete Your Quest

Present information about the strengths and weaknesses of one leading industry.

Name _____ Date _____

Strengths and Weaknesses

Use the following questions to help guide your research about the strengths and weaknesses in your industry.

Strengths

What are the goods or services the industry provides?

_____

Why do consumers buy the goods and services produced in the industry?

_____

What resources does the industry need?

_____

What advantages does the industry have over competitors?

_____

Weaknesses

What can the industry do better?

_____

What do competitors do better?

_____

What are the challenges the industry faces?

_____

Name _____ Date _____

The Nation's Strongest Industry

Circle the industry you think will be the strongest in ten years.

Agriculture

Manufacturing and Technology

Transportation

Healthcare

Real Estate

Support Your Answer:

Does the industry rely on natural resources that could become scarce? _____

Will people continue to need the goods or services that this industry provides? _____

Explain why you think the _____ industry will be the strongest in ten years.

_____

_____

_____

_____

Quick Activities

Industries of the World

Whole Class 25 minutes

Materials: Student Activity Mat 5B The World Outline, chart paper

Inform the class that the United States is one of the top economies in the world. It has a lot to offer across many different industries. However, it is not the only place in the world that produces or makes items.

Ask students to list three to four goods produced in the United States. As a class, use an Internet search engine to locate information on top producers of the selected goods.

Invite students to use Student Activity Mat 5B The World Outline. Have students identify on the map where each good is made. For each good, have students write the name of the country and the name of the good in the correct location on the map.

Entrepreneur

Individuals 30 minutes

Materials: Blackline Master: Business Model

Students create a business model for a product or service they would like to produce or provide.

Discuss the decisions made in starting a successful business:

- Do we have the resources needed to succeed?

- Do we need a lot of capital resources to start the business?

- Will we have to make a lot of trade-offs to succeed?

- Will the costs be greater than the benefits?

Distribute the blackline master **Business Model.** Allow students time to share and discuss their models.

Past and Present

Materials: Graphic Organizer: Venn Diagram, classroom or Library Media Center resources

Students create a Venn diagram showing a selected industry in the past and present.

Group students into research groups for each category: Agriculture, Manufacturing and Technology, Transportation, Healthcare, and Real Estate. Instruct groups to find a picture of their industry from 1900 and one from 2000.

Instruct groups to have a discussion about how the industry has changed in 100 years. Have them think about the ways natural, human, and capital resources were used to produce goods and services. Ask students if these uses have improved today.

Distribute the graphic organizer Venn Diagram. Instruct groups to paste the pictures inside the Venn diagram and to fill in the diagram with information on how the industry has changed.

🔵ELL Support for English Language Learners

Writing Review how to create precise and detailed sentences that connect ideas.

Entering: Have students draw pictures showing two ways the industry has changed. For example, the agricultural industry today might use trucks and airplanes to transport goods. Have students label the two pictures (for example, trucks, airplanes). Then have them use the word *and* to connect the pictures.

Emerging: Ask students to write two ways the industry has changed from 1900 to 2000. Have students work with partners to state these ways using only one sentence. Then have students write the compound sentence using *and, but,* or *so.* Provide examples if needed: "The healthcare industry has changed due to new kinds of medicine and new ways to treat illnesses."

Developing: Ask students to write one way their industry has changed and why the change was important for the industry to succeed. Have students work with partners to state facts using only one detailed sentence. Then have students write the detailed sentence. For example, "The healthcare industry has changed due to new kinds of medicine, which has saved lives and provided jobs."

Expanding: Ask students to write two details to support the claim: "Change can be for the better." Have students work with partners. Model making connections between facts and joining ideas into one sentence. For example, "The healthcare industry changed for the better so people now live longer, healthier lives."

Bridging: Have students write a paragraph about their chosen industry. Have them include a topic sentence and three sentences with details. After they have finished, have them work with a partner to revise the paragraph. Encourage students to look for ways to combine sentences or ideas in their paragraph.

Business Model

The good or service my business will provide is _____.

Draw a picture of the good or service to be provided:

Natural Resources
Needed:

Human Resources
Needed:

Capital Resources
Needed:

Explain your business. What are some things to think about to ensure that your business will be successful?

_____

_____

_____

Three generations of orange growers are sitting around a table discussing how to grow their family business using social media.

The Parts
- **Granddad**
- **Grandma**
- **Mom**
- **Dad**
- **Sarah**

Director's Notes:

The family is enjoying a meal together, sipping orange juice while looking over their small orange grove.

Granddad: Look at how far we've come. I started this orange grove with a handful of seeds, hopes, and dreams.

Grandma: And you've made a family business that has been passed down through several generations. Now it will be passed to our granddaughter, Sarah.

Sarah: I'm older now, and I am happy to be a part of the business.

Granddad: Times sure have changed. I remember how we could just set up a stand outside our house. We would get hundreds of customers to stop and buy baskets of our sweet, juicy oranges.

Dad: That's not how it works anymore, Pop! We had to stop selling roadside years ago and start selling in local supermarkets.

Mom: Remember the year we all celebrated because we saw our family label in all the grocery stores in the state? That was something!

Sarah: Well, if we want our business to continue growing, we must change things up a bit.

Granddad: Change? We haven't changed anything about how we plant, grow, or harvest our oranges. Why do we have to keep on changing? What's wrong with selling our oranges right here to the good people in our state?

Mom: You know that we have changed how we plant, grow, and harvest our oranges. We went from the few trees you started with to hundreds of orange trees in our small grove. In order to stay in the game, like so many of our competitors, we should change with the times.

Sarah: Mom is right. I am not talking about changing EVERYTHING. I think we should put ourselves on social media for sure.

Granddad: Hmph! I don't want to be like those ridiculous people on reality TV.

Dad: Dad, Sarah isn't suggesting we have a reality TV show about growing oranges. I think she means we need to get our faces and name out there on the Internet. We should have a social media page at least.

Mom: Exactly. We need to take online orders and ship gift baskets around the country. Gift baskets are always popular!

Granddad: I really wish we could just keep doing things the way we have been!

Sarah: Don't worry, Granddad, I won't be changing anything important like our family's promise to grow and sell the most delicious, juiciest oranges without using pesticides. I just want to spread our family's name and promise of hard work to others. I will set up a Web site and include online ordering. I will also set up a social media account, so we can post pictures of how we grow, care for, and harvest our oranges. I will make our hard work come to life with social media.

Dad: That's a great idea, Sarah. Everyone we know is posting and chatting on the Internet. If we want our business to grow and survive for future generations, we need to tell our story. We need to share our experiences with the world, and social media is the way to go!

Granddad: What ever happened to picking up the Sunday paper and seeing a snapshot of a family proud of their harvest?

Sarah: It's not in a newspaper anymore, Granddad, but people will still see a snapshot of a family who has worked hard and stayed together through easy and hard times. They will see it on social media. Times are changing, but our family values haven't.

Mom: Cheers to that! Here's to change and to all our future orange growers.

Granddad: Let's tell the world our story! Let's do it!

3 Let Freedom Ring

Objectives

- Read to learn about the British acts: Quartering Act, Stamp Tax Act, Townshend Acts, Coercive Acts.
- Identify the emotions stirred within the colonists by the passing of these acts.
- Create a timeline of events.
- Write a persuasive speech.

Quest Document-Based Writing: Write a Persuasive Speech

	Description	Duration	Materials	Participants
STEP 1 Set the Stage	Read a blackline master as an introduction to the Quest.	5 minutes	**Blackline Master:** Quest Kick Off	Whole Class
STEP 2 Launch the Activities	Watch a video with background information.		**Video:** Jamestown	
Activity 1 Soldier Says	Read about the Quartering Act and discuss its effect on the colonists.	30 minutes	**Blackline Master:** Quartering Act	Whole Class
Activity 2 Shop—No, Stop	Participate in a role play about the Stamp Act and Townshend Acts.	45 minutes	**Blackline Master:** Stamp Act, **Blackline Master:** Townshend Acts, "colony coins" (paper coins or tokens), envelopes	Whole Class
Activity 3 Create a Timeline	Read about the Boston Tea Party and Coercive Acts and create a timeline of events leading to the First Continental Congress.	30 minutes	**Blackline Master:** The Colonists Strike Back, sentence strips	Individuals
Activity 4 Give Me Liberty	Analyze a primary source.	30 minutes	**Primary Source:** Patrick Henry's Speech at First Continental Congress, highlighters (1 per student)	Small Groups
STEP 3 ELL Complete the Quest Write a Persuasive Speech	Write a speech to persuade undecided colonists to join the Revolution.	30 minutes	**Student Activity Mat:** 4B Quest	Individuals
Answer the **Compelling Question**	Discuss the compelling question.	10 minutes		Whole Class

Quick Activities

	Description	Duration	Materials	Participants
Match the Act	Cut and paste to match the British act with its description.	15 minutes	**Blackline Master:** Match the Act, **Quest Blackline Masters:** Quartering Act, Stamp Act, Townshend Acts, The Colonists Strike Back	Individuals
Write a Secret Letter	Write a letter in invisible ink.	15 minutes	cornstarch, hot plate, toothpicks (1 per student), sponge (1 piece per student), iodine, water	Individuals
Illustrate a Poem ELL	Read and illustrate a poem.	20 minutes	**Blackline Master:** The Midnight Ride of Paul Revere, poster paper, art supplies	Small Groups
Create an Advertisement	Write and illustrate an advertisement for the Revolution.	20 minutes	**Quest Blackline Masters:** Quartering Act, Stamp Act, Townshend Acts, The Colonists Strike Back; **Student Activity Mat:** 4A Who, What, Where in the United States?, poster paper, art supplies	Small Groups
Readers Theater	Perform a Readers Theater based on the First Continental Congress.	15 minutes	**Readers Theater:** First Continental Congress	Small Groups

Document-Based Writing: Let Freedom Ring

Compelling Question Why should America be free?

Welcome to Quest 3, Let Freedom Ring. In this Quest, students will learn about the British acts that moved the colonists toward Revolution. After participating in the Quest Activities, students will be prepared to discuss the compelling question at the end of this inquiry.

Objectives

- Read to learn about the British acts: Quartering Act, Stamp Act, Townshend Acts, Coercive Acts.
- Identify the emotions stirred within the colonists by the passing of these acts.
- Create a timeline of events.
- Write a persuasive speech.

STEP 1 Set the Stage ⏱ **5** minutes

Begin the Quest by distributing the blackline master **Quest Kick Off.** It will bring the world of the Quest to life, introducing a story to interest students and a mission to motivate them.

Story

This Quest takes students into the past to imagine themselves as colonists who are being affected by the passage of British acts.

· ·

Mission

Students are asked to imagine themselves as Patriots, committed to revolution and independence for America. Students must use what they've learned about the effects of British rule to write a persuasive speech to persuade colonists who are undecided to join forces in the fight for independence.

STEP 2 Launch the Activities

The following four activities will help students prepare for their persuasive speech by learning the reasons why colonists revolted against British rule. Note that all four can be done independently of the larger Quest.

Begin by showing the chapter video Jamestown, which will give students the content background they need to complete the activities.

Activity 1 Soldier Says **minutes**

Materials: Blackline Master: Quartering Act

Explain to students that as colonists they are still subject to British rule, even though they are technically in a separate place. Tell students that England has recently passed a new act which will affect the colonists, and it is up to the colonists to learn about this act so that they will understand the rule they must follow.

Distribute the blackline master **Quartering Act,** which provides an explanation of the act and how it affects the colonists. Have students read the information and use the spaces on the blackline master to answer the questions about the act.

To culminate, have students participate in a role play. Tell students to imagine that their desks are their houses, and that troops have just arrived that will need quartering. Bring in another class of students, and tell your students they must hand over anything that the other students need as long as they say, "Soldier Says." Have the visiting students spend a few moments demanding to sit at your students' desks and touching their pencils and books before leaving. Tell your students to talk with a partner about how this action made them feel. Instruct students to make notes on the back of their blackline master to describe their feelings at this forced, legal invasion.

Activity 2 Shop—No, Stop (45) minutes

Materials: Blackline Master: Stamp Act, Blackline Master: Townshend Acts, "colony coins" (paper coins or tokens, 5 per student), envelopes (1 per student)

Before the lesson begins, place an envelope with three "colony coins" at each student's desk. Tell students not to open the envelope until told.

Tell students that you've just learned of two new acts that will affect them as colonists. Remind students that even though they are separate from England, they are still under British rule and must follow these rules.

Distribute the blackline masters **Stamp Act** and **Townshend Acts,** which provide explanations of the acts and how they affect the colonists. Have students read the information and use the spaces on the blackline masters to answer the questions about the acts.

Next tell students to take out their colony coins and think about what colonists would buy with the money they had. On the board, make a price list of items, such as: cloth—3 coins, tea—2 coins, food—2 coins, paint—3 coins. Tell students to make a list of what they will buy. Have a volunteer come to "spend" the coins by stating what he or she will buy. Then remind the students of implications of the new acts—they must pay taxes on papers used in the lesson as well as additional taxes on items purchased. Take two coins from each student and remind them that they will now also have to pay an additional tax on their purchase. Have students talk in a small group about how these taxes affected their ability to purchase the things they needed. Instruct students to make notes on the back of the blackline masters about how each act affected them and how they felt at the hands of this forced loss of income.

Activity 3   Create a Timeline   (30) minutes

Materials: Blackline Master: The Colonists Strike Back, sentence strips

Explain to students that the colonists were finally fed up with all these taxes. They showed their rebellion with the Boston Tea Party. But explain that their rebellion came with a cost—more acts called the Coercive Acts. Define the word *coercive* as something done by force or threat. Explain that the colonists knew the British were trying to punish them by creating and enforcing these acts. Explain to students that the colonists referred to the Coercive Acts as the "Intolerable Acts," because they had reached the point where they could no longer tolerate British rule. The Boston Tea Party started a momentum that would lead up to the meeting of the First Continental Congress.

Distribute the blackline masters **The Colonists Strike Back,** which provide explanations of the Boston Tea Party and the successive acts that were passed as a result. Have students read the information and use the spaces on the blackline masters to answer the questions about the acts.

Pass out sentence strips and instruct students to use the strips to create a timeline of events, beginning with the Boston Tea Party and ending with the First Continental Congress. Tell students to create a tick mark on the timeline to note each act in the Coercive Acts. For each mark, have students write the name of the act and the date.

Activity 4   Give Me Liberty   (30) minutes

Materials: Primary Source: Patrick Henry's Speech at First Continental Congress, highlighters (1 per student)

Remind students that a primary source is an account of events given by someone who experienced them firsthand. Explain that Patrick Henry was a member of the First Continental Congress, and that his moving speech has come to be symbolic of the start of the American Revolution.

Distribute the primary source Patrick Henry's Speech at First Continental Congress. Tell students to first read the speech all the way through. Pass out a highlighter to each student. Divide students into small groups. Have the groups highlight and discuss the words and phrases used within the speech that elicit emotion (such as the final line "give me liberty or give me death!"). Have students discuss the effects of using emotional language in persuasive writing.

Part 1 Write a Persuasive Speech ⏱30 minutes

Materials: Student Activity Mat 4B Quest

Remind students of the unfair treatment that the colonists received at the hand of British rule. Instruct students to review the blackline masters used in the activities to remind themselves of each of the acts and the effects these acts had on the colonists.

Have students draft their persuasive speeches. Remind students that in order to persuade a reader or listener's opinion, the writer must present facts with reasons and supporting evidence.

Finally, have students use Student Activity Mat 4B Quest to respond to questions about the Quest for this lesson.

🔵 Support for English Language Learners

Writing Remind students of the actions taken by the British that harmed the colonists. On the board, write the name of each act, the effect it had on the colonists, and why this effect was harmful.

Entering: Have students draw and label a picture of one reason why an undecided colonist should agree with the idea of revolution.

Emerging: Have students draw a picture of one reason why an undecided colonist should agree with the idea of revolution. Then have students write to complete the sentence frame: *You should join the revolution because* _____.

Developing: Have students complete a two-part explanation of why an undecided colonist should join the revolution using the sentence frames: *The British harmed the colonists by* _____. *This is unfair to colonists because* _____.

Expanding: Have students complete a two-part explanation of why an undecided colonist should join the revolution by providing an explanation of an action of the British and its effects on the colonists.

Bridging: Have students complete an explanation of why an undecided colonist should join the revolution by providing a detailed explanation of at least two actions of the British and how colonists were negatively affected by British actions.

After students finish writing their persuasive speeches, encourage them to reflect on what they learned. As a class, discuss the compelling question for this Quest "Why should America be free?"

Students have learned about the acts passed by the British and the effects of these acts on the American colonists. They should use what they learned to answer the compelling question.

Quest Kick Off

Let Freedom Ring

You've joined the ranks of other freedom-minded colonists as a Patriot. But it will take many Patriots working together in order to win independence for America. In order to succeed you'll need to convince other colonists to join you in demanding freedom from England. There are plenty of reasons for joining you, the Patriots, but you'll have to point these reasons out in order to win support from these undecided colonists.

Your Mission

Learn about the British acts that drove the colonists to rebellion. Then use what you've learned to write a persuasive speech. Your persuasive speech must include reasons and evidence that will convince undecided colonists to join you in your fight for freedom from British rule.

To write your persuasive speech:

Activity 1 **Soldier Says:** Examine the Quartering Act and enact its effect on the colonists.

Activity 2 **Shop—No, Stop:** Analyze the Stamp Tax Act and Townshend Acts and perform a role play.

Activity 3 **Create a Timeline:** Read to learn about the Boston Tea Party and Coercive Acts and create a timeline of events leading up to the First Continental Congress.

Activity 4 **Give Me Liberty:** Explore the impact of a primary source speech on the colonists.

Complete Your Quest

Write a persuasive speech to convince undecided colonists to support the Revolution.

Quartering Act

The Quartering Act was a British law passed in 1765.
The law forced American colonists to provide food, supplies,
and housing to members of the British army who were
stationed in the colonies. This law meant that American
colonists had no choice in providing these things for the
British soldiers, even if the colonists were in need of the food
or supplies themselves. The colonists viewed this act as
one of oppression. It was peacetime, and the British troops
were in place in the colonies only to ensure the colonists
were following British laws and paying British taxes. To the
colonists, this act was a way of reminding them that the
British were in charge.

Answer the questions about the Quartering Act.

Who? _____

What? _____

When? _____

Where? _____

Why? _____

Name _____ Date _____

Stamp Act

The Stamp Act was passed by the British Parliament (government) in 1765, at nearly the same time as the Quartering Act. This act placed a tax on all legal documents, newspapers, and pamphlets. At a time before Internet, television, or even radio, paper was a very valuable means of sending and receiving information, and the British government knew that. The colonists viewed this act as a way for Britain to gain money from their need to access information. This act placed a huge and unfair burden on the colonists, and they reacted with protests. Patriots Patrick Henry and Samuel Adams created the "Sons of Liberty" as a way of fighting back against British injustice. This secret group protested British laws and taxes that were unfair to the colonists.

Answer the questions about the Stamp Act.

Who? _____

What? _____

When? _____

Where? _____

Why? _____

Townshend Acts

The Townshend Acts were passed in 1767 as a way to gain more money from the colonists through taxation. These acts created new taxes on imported goods from Britain (things that the colonists bought that came from Britain). The colonists relied heavily on these imported goods, and these taxes affected them greatly. They now had to pay even more money for things like paper, lead, glass, paint, and even tea. The Townshend Acts also set up a specialized department, called the American Customs Board, to collect these taxes. British officials now had the right to search the homes or businesses of colonists. Anyone who was caught smuggling, or not paying taxes on these goods, would be tried in an American court reigned by British rule.

Answer the questions about the Townshend Acts.

Who? _____

What? _____

When? _____

Where? _____

Why? _____

The Colonists Strike Back

On December 16, 1773, the colonists had endured enough.

They struck back in one of the most well-known protests leading up to the American Revolution. The Boston Tea Party came about due to another British tax: The Tea Act. Tea was a favorite drink of the colonists, and the British knew that. In this act, they raised the taxes on tea and stated that the colonists were only allowed to purchase tea from the East India Tea Company, a company owned by the British. The colonists refused to pay the tax and told Britain to take their tea back, but the British refused and left the tea on the ship, stating the colonists must pay. On the night of December 16, the colonists boarded the three ships and tossed 342 chests (90,000 pounds) of tea into the ocean in protest. In today's dollars, that amounted to over one million dollars' worth of tea.

Answer the questions about the Boston Tea Party.

Who? _____

What? _____

When? _____

Where? _____

Why? _____

The Coercive Acts

In 1774, British Parliament passed five acts in order to punish the colonists for the Boston Tea Party.

- Boston Port Act: Closed the port of Boston until the colonists paid for the tea they had ruined.

- Massachusetts Government Act: Gave more power to the governor, who was appointed by British rule, and took governing power away from colonists.

- Administration of Justice Act: Allowed government officials who were accused of wrongdoing to be tried in Britain instead of in the colonies.

- Quartering Act, 1774: Expanded on the original Quartering Act by forcing colonies to provide barracks (groups of buildings for military housing). If barracks were not built, the act gave soldiers the right to take the colonists' homes.

- Quebec Act: Expanded British Canadian territory into the Ohio Valley and made Quebec a Catholic province.

The passage of these acts led to the assembly of the First Continental Congress, the first step in America's path to independence.

Answer the questions about the Coercive Acts.

Who? _____

What? _____

When? _____

Where? _____

Why? _____

Patrick Henry's Speech at First Continental Congress

There is no longer any room for hope. If we wish to be free, we must fight! I repeat it, sir, we must fight!

It is in vain, sir, to **extenuate**[1] the matter. Gentlemen may cry, Peace, Peace, but there is no peace. The war is actually begun! The next gale that sweeps from the north will bring to our ears the clash of resounding arms! Our brethren are already in the field! Why stand we here idle? What is it that gentlemen wish? What would they have? Is life so dear, or peace so sweet, as to be purchased at the price of chains and slavery? Forbid it, Almighty God! I know not what course others may take; but as for me, give me liberty or give me death!

---

[1]extenuate: forgive, make light of a serious situation

Quick Activities

Match the Act

Individuals 15 minutes

Materials: Blackline Master: Match the Act, Quest Blackline Masters: Quartering Act, Stamp Act, Townshend Acts, The Colonists Strike Back

If students did not participate in the Quest Activities, have them read the blackline master fact sheets to learn about the acts passed by the British that affected the colonists.

Distribute the blackline master, **Match the Act,** which provides students with the names and descriptions of the British acts.

Have students cut out the names of the acts and glue them to correctly match the name of the act with its description.

Write a Secret Letter

Individuals 15 minutes

Materials: cornstarch, hot plate, toothpicks (1 per student), sponge (1 piece per student), iodine, water

Explain to students that sending letters to family in England could be difficult with all the talk of revolution in America. One way colonists could protect themselves was by sending secret letters. Explain that sending secret letters was a tactic that was later used by the American Army during the Revolutionary War.

Follow these steps to have students practice writing their own secret letters. First, mix 4 teaspoons of water with 2 tablespoons of cornstarch, and stir the mixture until smooth. Heat and stir the mixture over a hot plate for several minutes. Allow each student to dip a toothpick into the mixture and write an invisible message on a piece of paper. Let the paper dry. Have students dip a piece of sponge into a solution of 1 teaspoon iodine and 10 teaspoons of water and carefully wipe the paper with the sponge. The message should turn purple.

Illustrate a Poem

Materials: Blackline Master: The Midnight Ride of Paul Revere, poster paper, art supplies

Give students the following background information on Paul Revere and his famous ride: *Paul Revere was a patriot, or a person who strongly supported American independence. He was an active member of the Sons of Liberty, a group of patriots devoted to independence for the colonies. In April of 1775, British troops were in Boston, Massachusetts. There was a rumor that trouble was ahead. But Paul Revere and the Sons of Liberty were ready. They rode away on horseback, hoping to reach the colonists before the British troops. Paul Revere and the Sons of Liberty's early warning gave the colonists precious time to prepare for the upcoming attack.*

Divide students into small groups and distribute the blackline master **The Midnight Ride of Paul Revere** which contains an excerpt of the poem.

Read the poem aloud chorally and have a brief discussion to explain the times and phrases used in the poem. Then have student groups discuss the events of the poem. Give each group a sheet of poster paper and art supplies, and have them decide on the best way to illustrate the poem. Instruct students to cut and paste the poem within the created illustration. At the end of the activity, collect all illustrations and bind them together to create a book. Place the book in the classroom library for students to read.

....

Support for English Language Learners

Reading and Speaking Explain to students that events in a text have an order that they follow, and that this order is called a sequence of events. Have the students practice identifying events in sequential order in text by participating in the following activities.

Entering: Read the poem aloud to students. Have students draw to illustrate a scene and label it as first, middle, or last.

Emerging: Have students read the poem aloud with you. Then have students retell the events in the poem by answering questions about what happened first, next, then, and last.

Developing: Have students read the poem aloud. Then have students retell the events of the poem to you in sequential order.

Expanding: Have students read the poem aloud. Then have students explain the succession of events within the poem to a small group.

Bridging: Have students read the poem. Then have students retell the poem to the class, explaining how each event in the poem successively builds toward the ending.

Create an Advertisement

Materials: Quest Blackline Masters: Quartering Act, Stamp Act, Townshend Acts, The Colonists Strike Back; Student Activity Mat 4A Who, What, Where in the United States?; poster paper, art supplies

If students did not participate in the Quest Activities, have them read the blackline master fact sheets to learn about the acts passed by the British that affected the colonists.

Have students use Student Activity Mat 4A Who, What, Where in the United States? to compile information about people, places, and events connected with the acts imposed.

Have students use poster paper and art supplies to create an advertisement to garner support for the American Revolution. Instruct students to use reasons from their research in their advertisement.

First Continental Congress

Materials: Readers Theater: First Continental Congress

Tell students that Readers Theater is a time for them to enjoy a role-playing situation centered around the topic of each chapter.

If students are unfamiliar with Readers Theater scripts, provide a brief explanation of the elements present in a Readers Theater. Point out the different roles, dialogue, and the director's notes. If necessary, explain to students that the dialogue are the words or lines spoken by the characters. Explain that the director's notes give information about the play that isn't in the dialogue. Tell students that as they perform the Readers Theater they should read with accuracy, appropriate rate, and expression.

Name _____ Date _____

Match the Act

Read the descriptions. Cut the boxes containing the titles from the bottom of the page and paste them to match to the correct description.

	A series of acts passed by British Parliament in order to punish the colonists for the Boston Tea Party.
	Forced colonists to provide food, housing, and supplies to British soldiers stationed in the colonies.
	Assembly in which colonists agreed to begin working toward independence for America.
	Placed new taxes on paper goods in the colonies.
	Placed increased taxes on goods that were imported from Britain.
	Protest led by colonists in which 342 chests of tea were thrown into Boston Harbor.

Quartering Act	Stamp Act	Townshend Acts
Boston Tea Party	Coercive Acts	First Continental Congress

The Midnight Ride of Paul Revere

Read the excerpt from "Paul Revere's Ride" by
Henry Wadsworth Longfellow.

Listen, my children, and you shall hear

Of the midnight ride of Paul Revere,

On the eighteenth of April, in Seventy-Five:

Hardly a man is now alive

Who remembers that famous day and year.

He said to his friend, "If the British march

By land or sea from the town to-night,

Hang a lantern aloft in the belfry-arch

Of the North-Church-tower, as a signal-light,—

One if by land, and two if by sea;

And I on the opposite shore will be,

Ready to ride and spread the alarm

Through every Middlesex village and farm,

For the country-folk to be up and to arm."

In this Readers Theater, you will act out the meeting of the First Continental Congress as they discuss beginning a revolution.

The Parts

4 players:

- Colonial delegate 1 (CD 1)
- Colonial delegate 2 (CD 2)
- Colonial delegate 3 (CD 3)
- Colonial delegate 4 (CD 4)

Director's Notes:

The four players stand, facing one another, as the conversation begins.

CD 1: Thank you for traveling to this meeting. We have some important things to discuss.

CD 2: Indeed we do, Sir. Let's get to work.

CD 3: We must make some difficult decisions today about our response to the injustices we are facing.

CD 4: We can no longer sit back and wait for the Parliament to do what's right for us. They are proving every day that they are not interested in our well-being.

CD 1:	It certainly seems that way.
CD 2:	Yes, it does. More taxes, more taxes, more taxes! Nothing but taxes and punishment for us.
CD 3:	We know this is wrong. But what can we do about it?
CD 4:	We can fight back!
CD 1:	I don't know if fighting is the right answer.
CD 2:	Well what else are we going to do?
CD 3:	We can't just cave in and follow these laws. We're servants to them now. They're taking our money, our land, even our homes!
CD 4:	We must stand for it no longer!
CD 1:	If we fight, we could be seriously harmed. This could become war.
CD 2:	I think it *will* become war. They will not give in easily. Will our fellow colonists want this?
CD 3:	Is life under this oppressive British rule better?

CD 3 pauses. All 4 CDs shake their heads no.

CD 4:	We must do what is best for all. We must fight.
CD 1:	I agree. We must bring freedom to America.
All 3: *raising a fist in air*	Let freedom ring!

Government, Landmarks, and Symbols

Objectives

- Identify and describe the differences between the rights and responsibilities of citizens.
- Explain the purpose of the U.S. Constitution and why it is important today.
- Write a class constitution that follows a ratification process.

Quest Collaborative Discussion: Create a Class Constitution

	Description	Duration	Materials	Participants
STEP 1 Set the Stage	Read a blackline master as an introduction to the project.	15 minutes	**Blackline Master:** Quest Kick Off	Whole Class
STEP 2 Launch the Activities	Watch a video with background information.	5 minutes	**Leveled Readers:** What Are Rules?; A Day Without Rules; Our Constitution at Work **Video:** Independence Hall	Whole Class
Activity 1 Right or Responsibility?	Create a comic strip that shows good citizens.	40 minutes	**Blackline Master:** Drawing a Good Citizen	Individuals
Activity 2 We the People	Make a booklet of the Preamble to the Constitution.	30 minutes	**Blackline Master:** Preamble Cards	Individuals
Activity 3 We the Students	Create a preamble for the class constitution.	30 minutes	chart paper	Whole Class
Activity 4 Bill of Rights	Read and illustrate amendments from the Bill of Rights.	40 minutes	**Blackline Master:** Bill of Rights	Small Groups
STEP 3 Complete the Quest The Path to Ratification	Propose rules for the class constitution.	40 minutes	**Blackline Master:** An Idea for a Class Rule	Small Groups
Collaborative **ELL** Discussion	Vote to finalize rules for the class constitution.	45 minutes	**Blackline Master:** An Idea for a Class Rule (completed) Class Preamble, flip chart paper	Whole Class
Answer the **Compelling Question**	Discuss what makes a good rule.	20 minutes		Whole Class

Quick Activities

	Description	Duration	Materials	Participants
Symbols of America and My State	Draw a visual explaining a symbol.	30 minutes	**Blackline Master:** My State Symbols **Graphic Organizer:** Web American symbols, chart paper	Small Groups
Branches of Government	Compose a song explaining the three branches of government.	25 minutes	**Blackline Master:** Three Branches of Government **Student Activity Mat 3A:** Graphic Organizer	Partners
Local Versus State Government	Create a Venn diagram to compare local and state governments.	30 minutes	**Student Activity Mat 1A:** United States, Physical **Graphic Organizer:** Venn Diagram	Individuals
Dear Mayor ELL	Write a letter to your mayor for a community improvement project.	30 minutes	**Blackline Master:** A Letter to the Mayor	Individuals
Readers Theater: Little Pig and Mr. Wolf	Perform a script about a trial for destruction of property.	30 minutes	**Blackline Master:** Little Pig and Mr. Wolf	Whole Class

Collaborative Discussion: Create a Class Constitution

 **Compelling Question** ## What makes a good rule?

Welcome to Quest 4, Create a Class Constitution. In this Quest, your students will present and vote on rules to create a class constitution. This inquiry simulates government lawmaking and the ratification of the U.S. Constitution on a micro level, while also preparing students to address the compelling question at the end of this inquiry.

Objectives

• Identify and describe the differences between the rights and responsibilities of citizens.

• Explain the purpose of the U.S. Constitution and why it is important today.

• Write a class constitution that follows a ratification process.

STEP 1 Set the Stage ⏱ 15 minutes

Begin the Quest by distributing the blackline master **Quest Kick Off.** This introduces a real-world dilemma for students to solve and presents a story and mission to motivate them.

Story

Imagine that your classroom is like a new country. There may already be some rules for your "classroom nation," but what new rules should be added? Your students must develop and agree on rules for your classroom to be safe, respectful, and successful.

Mission

Your students will work together to write a classroom constitution. Students will focus on understanding their rights and responsibilities while also considering how to develop reasonable rules and strategies for amending their rules in the future.

STEP 2 Launch the Activities

The following four activities will help students create their classroom constitution by researching the subject matter to create a strong set of class rules. Note that all four can be done independently of the larger Quest.

Begin by showing the chapter video, Independence Hall. Help students compare the national government to the workings of their own classroom. After the video, discuss the rules a country may have for its citizens and why these rules exist. Then discuss why classroom rules exist. You may also assign the appropriate Leveled Reader for this chapter.

Activity 1 Right or Responsibility? minutes

Materials: Blackline Master: Drawing a Good Citizen

Students will create a comic strip that demonstrates good citizenship in the school community.

Distribute the blackline master **Drawing a Good Citizen.** Work with students to define the term *good citizen. A good citizen is someone who makes the community a better place for themselves and others.* Point out how a *right* is a freedom that is protected by laws. A *responsibility* is something you should do, or a duty.

Before reading the comic strip, spend time discussing that good citizens have responsibilities. Then discuss how rules and laws are made so that we can all better understand how to be good citizens of our classroom, town, city, state, and country.

Finally, read through the comic strip as a class. Then instruct students to create a comic strip that shows behaviors of a good citizen in the school community.

Activity 2 | **We the People** (30) minutes

Materials: Blackline Master: Preamble Cards, Leveled Readers

Students create preamble booklets by cutting out illustrations and text for each section of the preamble.

Before you begin, ask students, "What is the U.S. Constitution, and why is it important to you?" Allow students to share their ideas. Discuss how the Constitution protects the rights, freedoms, justice, and equality of all American citizens. You may wish to read aloud *A More Perfect Union: The Story of Our Constitution* by Betsy and Giulio Maestro.

Read the preamble aloud to the class. Discuss the terms *liberty, justice,* and *equality*. Then reread the preamble, stopping line by line to ask students what each line means.

Distribute the blackline master **Preamble Cards,** which students will use to understand the purpose of the Constitution and construct their version of the preamble. Instruct students to cut out the preamble cards. Students can then place the cards in sequence to form a booklet. (Help students staple, tie, or clip the cards together to form a booklet.)

As an alternative to this activity, students can cut out the cards and play a matching game to place together the cards that mean the same thing.

Ask students again, "Why is the U.S. Constitution an important document?"

Activity 3 We the Students (30) minutes

Materials: chart paper

In this activity, the class creates a preamble for their class constitution.

Continue the conversation about the importance of the U.S. Constitution. Explain how the Constitution focuses on liberty, justice, and equality. Place students into small groups, and have them list three main categories for their class constitution (for example, safety, order, and respect). You may want to make a longer list of categories on the board for students to choose from.

Lead the class in a shared writing experience to create a preamble for the class constitution. Present the following as a sample for the class:

We the students of Class xxxx

In order to form a more perfect learning space

Establish (fairness)

Ensure a positive culture

Provide order

Promote respectful speech

And safety

To ourselves and our belongings

Do ordain and establish this constitution

For the Third Grade Students of Class xxxx

Activity 4 Bill of Rights (40) minutes

Materials: Blackline Master: Bill of Rights, Leveled Readers

Students discuss the amendments in the Bill of Rights.

Discuss the role of the Constitutional Convention. You may wish to read excerpts from *Shhh! We're Writing the Constitution* by Jean Fritz.

Make sure to emphasize that the Constitution would not have been accepted by the states if the Founders did not add the Bill of Rights. The new citizens of the United States of America wanted to make sure individual rights were protected.

Distribute the blackline master **Bill of Rights,** which simplifies the wording of the first ten amendments.

Inform students that the First Amendment gives Americans the following freedoms: freedom to practice or not to practice religion, freedom of speech, freedom of the press, and freedom to assemble.

The Second Amendment gives Americans the right to keep a firearm and protect themselves. Pair students and assign them three amendments to discuss.

Ask: "Why do you think some people in the late 1780s did not want to approve the Constitution without the Bill of Rights?"

Part 1 The Path to Ratification minutes

Materials: Blackline Master: An Idea for a Class Rule

Have students create rules to propose to the class during the classroom constitution discussion. Distribute the blackline master **An Idea for a Class Rule.**

Read the political cartoon: "United We Stand, Divided We Fall." Inform students that in order to ratify, or accept, the Constitution, nine out of the thirteen states needed to vote to approve it. In the fall of 1787, only five states were united and approved the Constitution. Point to the political cartoon and read the first five states (left to right). The eight remaining states were not as fast to approve the Constitution. Continue to read the states, noting how Rhode Island appears to be falling. The cartoon shows that the states needed to unite together to form a successful country. Rhode Island was the last state to approve the Constitution in 1790.

Group students into rule categories (for example, safety, order, respect). Each group will use the blackline master **An Idea for a Class Rule** to create a rule for the classroom constitution. Be sure they are prepared to support or make changes to their proposed rule so that the class can approve it.

Part 2 Collaborative Discussion minutes

Materials: completed Blackline Master: An Idea for a Class Rule, Class Preamble, flip chart paper

After students have completed their rule, have them participate in a class discussion and vote to finalize the rules for the class constitution.

Before they begin, discuss these rules:

1. Do not interrupt.

2. Listen carefully.

3. Speak clearly, but do not raise your voice or shout.

4. Do not make fun of others or say hurtful things.

5. Ask questions if you are unsure what something means.

Remind the class that this is a democratic process, so each rule will be voted upon. If the rule receives more yes votes than no votes, it will become part of the class constitution.

Have each group present a rule. Remind students to provide support for their rule while presenting it. Make sure each rule is discussed completely. If any rules need to be modified based on the discussion, have each group edit the rule on the blackline master. Once the rule has been accepted, write it onto a formal classroom constitution on flip chart paper. Hold a signing ceremony, and have each student sign the class constitution.

ⓔ Support for English Language Learners

Speaking As students prepare for the Collaborative Discussion, remind them to contribute and elaborate on the ideas in the discussion through listening, asking questions, using details to answer questions, and extending the conversation with their own thoughts. Have students practice having a discussion by conducting the following activities.

Entering: Have students draw a picture of one rule they have at home. (For example, putting the trash on the curb on Tuesdays, washing the dishes after a meal, or walking the dog.) Help students label their drawing.

Emerging: Have students use these sentence frames or sentence starters to talk about rules at home. _____ *takes out the trash on* _____. *At home, every morning I eat* _____. *To clean up after a meal, we* _____. *Some chores at home are* _____.

Developing: Divide students into pairs. Encourage one partner to name a rule from his or her home. Have the other partner ask a yes or no question about the rule. Provide examples if needed: "Do you have rules about cleaning?" "Do you have a lot of rules?" Then have the partners switch roles.

Expanding: Divide students into pairs. Encourage one partner to name a rule from his or her home. Have the other partner ask a question about the rule. Then have the partners switch roles.

Bridging: Divide students into pairs. Instruct students to have conversations about why they have rules at home. Encourage students to explain some rules at home and build onto one another's ideas with relevant information. As students converse, make sure they are asking and answering questions and following turn-taking rules appropriately.

Part 3 Answer the Compelling Question minutes

After students create their classroom constitution, encourage them to reflect on what they learned. As a class, discuss the compelling question for this Quest, "What makes a good rule?"

Students have learned about the rights and responsibilities of good citizens. They also learned about the purpose of the Constitution, including the ratification process, and the purpose of the Bill of Rights. They should use what they learned to answer the compelling question.

 **Kick Off** Name _____ Date _____

Create a Class Constitution

Imagine that your classroom is like a new country. There may already be some rules for your "classroom nation," but what new rules should be added? Act quickly to think of the rules everyone needs for the class to be safe, respectful, and successful. How will you agree on the class rules?

To prepare for the class discussion and vote, work with your team to do the following:

Activity 1 **Right or Responsibility?:** Create a short comic strip showing good citizenship in your school community.

Activity 2 **We the People:** Match the words of the preamble with their meanings.

Activity 3 **We the Students:** As a class, draft a preamble for your class constitution.

Activity 4 **Bill of Rights:** Read to understand the first ten amendments, and illustrate three amendments.

Complete Your Quest

Write rules for the class constitution and discuss the proposed rules as a class. Then vote to accept rules to be added to the class constitution.

Your Mission

Your classroom needs rules to be a safe, respectful, and successful place. Work with a small group to create a class constitution. Think carefully about the ways leaders develop rules. Remember, the rule you create must win the popular vote of your classmates!

Drawing a Good Citizen

Read the comic strip.

Activity 2

Preamble Cards

Cut out all ten cards on each page. Match each picture to the correct card. Place the cards in sequence. Staple or tie the cards together to make a preamble booklet.

Government, Landmarks, and Symbols   **66**   Quest Student Worksheet

We the People of the United States

In order to form a more perfect union

Establish justice

Insure domestic tranquility

Provide for the common defense

Promote the general welfare

And secure the blessings of liberty

To ourselves and our posterity

Do ordain and establish this constitution

For the United States of America

All the people in our country

Work together for a country that looks out for everyone

To be fair and honest

To live and work peacefully

To keep us safe and protected

To make sure people have food, a home, and safety

To protect our freedoms and express ourselves

To protect these rights for future Americans

To live by and follow this list of rules and promises

To be a document for our country

Bill of Rights

Read the first ten amendments. Then choose three more to illustrate.

First Amendment

Grants people freedom to practice any religion, to speak freely, to write freely, and to assemble peacefully.

Second Amendment

Gives a person the right to keep a firearm.

Third Amendment

Grants people the right to refuse to house soldiers in peacetime.

Fourth Amendment

A person cannot be arrested or have their property searched unless there is "probable cause" that they committed a crime.

Fifth Amendment
Provides rules for due process when a person has been charged with a crime.

Sixth Amendment
Gives a person the right to a fair and speedy trial.

Seventh Amendment
Gives people the right to a trial by jury.

Eighth Amendment
Protects people from unfair fines and cruel punishment.

Ninth Amendment
States that not every right is listed in the Constitution and that these unlisted rights are still protected.

Tenth Amendment
Gives the powers that are not given to the federal government to the states or the people.

Name _____ Date _____

An Idea for a Class Rule

Look at the political cartoon with your class. Discuss why it is important for people to agree about rules so that rules can work.

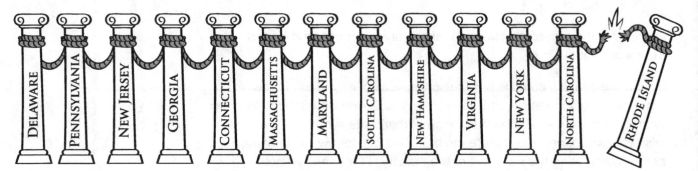

UNITED WE STAND

DIVIDED WE FALL

Columns labeled: DELAWARE, PENNSYLVANIA, NEW JERSEY, GEORGIA, CONNECTICUT, MASSACHUSETTS, MARYLAND, SOUTH CAROLINA, NEW HAMPSHIRE, VIRGINIA, NEW YORK, NORTH CAROLINA, RHODE ISLAND

Work in groups to answer the questions. Then create a rule for your class constitution. Think about the best way to write and present the rule so that your classmates understand, agree with, and vote to approve the rule.

What is your proposed rule?	
Why is it important to have this rule?	
Is this rule constitutional? Does this rule uphold our classroom principles of safety, order, or respect?	
What should be the consequence of breaking the rule?	
How likely is it that the class will ratify this rule? If the answer is "not likely," consider a new rule or reword the rule.	

Quick Activities

Symbols of America and My State

Small Groups minutes

Materials: Blackline Master: My State Symbols, Graphic Organizer: Web, images of symbols of the United States and your state, chart paper

In this activity, groups create a web about one symbol of the United States or your state.

Before the activity, compile pictures or replicas of any of the following: American flag, bald eagle, Statue of Liberty, U.S. Constitution, Declaration of Independence, your state flag, or any other state symbols. (You may wish to have students complete the blackline master **My State Symbols** before completing the next part of the activity.) Place the symbols and a piece of chart paper at different stations around the room.

Instruct students to walk around to each station and jot down ideas of what each symbol represents. Then review student ideas and provide fast facts about each symbol to the class.

Break the class into small groups (one group per symbol). Give each group books, printouts from Web pages, or other gathered resources to discover:

- what the symbol represents

- how the symbol was created

- why the symbol is important

Distribute copies of the graphic organizer **Web.** Have students organize the answers to these questions on the graphic organizer. Then allow groups to share their findings with the class.

Branches of Government

Materials: Blackline Master: Three Branches of Government, Student Activity Mat 3A Graphic Organizer

In this activity, partners create a song to teach younger students the basic functions of the three branches of government.

Distribute the blackline master **Three Branches of Government,** which explains the basic roles of each branch of government.

Review the main functions of the judicial (makes sure the laws follow the U.S. Constitution), legislative (writes the laws), and executive (carries out the laws) branches of government with the whole class. (Suggested resource: http://www.Kids.gov.)

Have students use Student Activity Mat 3A **Graphic Organizer** to write words or phrases related to each of the three branches of government. They can use these words or phrases to help write their song.

Last, invite pairs of students to write a song about the three branches of government using the tune of a popular song, such as "Three Blind Mice." Alternately, students can write a poem about the three branches of government.

Local Versus State Government

Individuals (30) **minutes**

Materials: Student Activity Mat 1A United States, Physical;
Graphic Organizer: Venn Diagram

Invite students to use Student Activity Mat 1A **United States, Physical** to identify their state capital. Then have students locate where they live and Washington, D.C. This will help them visualize where federal, state, and local governments operate.

Ask the class, "What is the difference between our local and our state governments?" Explain that government sets laws and provides services for the people. An elected official, usually a mayor, leads a town or city. The governor, also an elected official, leads the entire state. Explain that both forms of government set laws, help run communities, and provide services to people. For additional information visit: http://www.Kids.gov.

Distribute the graphic organizer **Venn Diagram.** Instruct students to label the left circle *local government* and the right circle *state government.* Have students use the Venn diagram to compare and contrast the roles of your local and state governments.

Dear Mayor

Individuals (30) **minutes**

Materials: Blackline Master: A Letter to the Mayor

Visit your city or county government Web site with your class. Explore services the government offers, including public programs that interest children. Remind students of the many responsibilities of the state and local governments. Be sure to talk about how the government runs state parks and beaches; helps to protect public land, water, plants, and animals; organizes and manages schools; runs state hospitals; and supports programs that assist people in need. Have students discuss the importance of these services.

Show students a picture of their mayor. As a class, brainstorm ideas that can improve their entire local community (i.e., new park, library, or programs for the homeless). Be sure to have students brainstorm things that a mayor might have the power to address.

Review with students how to write a letter. Instruct students to write a letter to the mayor with an idea on how to improve the local community. Students can use the blackline master **A Letter to the Mayor** to complete the letter or to use as guidance.

Support for English Language Learners

Writing Remind students that elaborating on ideas when writing helps the reader make connections among the ideas presented in the writing. Tell students that as they write their letters to the mayor they should use compound and complex sentences to elaborate on their ideas.

Entering: Invite students to draw a picture of an improvement they would like to see in their community. Help them label their drawing.

Emerging: Divide students into pairs. Write the sentences: *Rules are important to keep us safe. Rules provide order. Rules are important to keep us safe, and rules provide order.* Then ask students to circle the word used to combine the two shorter sentences.

Developing: Have students complete the following sentence frames to help them write their letter to the mayor. *We need ____ because ____. We need ____ and ____.*

Expanding: Divide students into pairs. Give students two independent clauses. Ask them to make connections between the two clauses and combine them using phrases such as *even though* or *because*. Example: We need new park equipment *because* the equipment is falling apart.

Bridging: Divide students into pairs. Give students a variety of sentence stems and instruct them to connect the stems in a variety of ways. Example: We need a cafe in the park, so parents can sit and talk while their kids play safely. Then ask students to write their own sentences.

Readers Theater: Little Pig and Mr. Wolf Whole Class (30) minutes

Materials: Blackline Master: Little Pig and Mr. Wolf

Before reading the Readers Theater, ensure all students are familiar with the tale "The Three Little Pigs." If you think some students might not know the story, use the following synopsis:

The Three Little Pigs
The Three Little Pigs each build a house. The first pig builds a house of straw. The second pig builds a house of sticks. The third pig builds a house of bricks.

The Big Bad Wolf wants to eat the pigs. He finds the first pig hiding inside the house of straw. He huffs and he puffs, and he blows the house down.

The first little pig runs away to the house of sticks. The two pigs hide inside. The Big Bad Wolf comes to the house of sticks. He huffs and he puffs, and he puffs and he huffs. He blows down the house of sticks.

The two pigs run to the house of bricks, where all three pigs now hide inside. The wolf comes to the house of bricks. No matter how hard he tries, he cannot blow down the house of bricks. The three little pigs are safe from the big, bad wolf.

Three Branches of Government

Judicial Branch
The Supreme Court—
made up of nine justices—
makes sure laws follow the
United States Constitution.

Legislative Branch
The Senate and
House of Representatives
make the laws.

Executive Branch
The president
and members
of the cabinet
carry out the
laws.

Name _____ Date _____

A Letter to the Mayor

Your Address: _____

City: _____ State _____ ZIP Code _____

Date: _____

Mayor's Name: _____

Mayor's Address: _____

City: _____ State _____ ZIP Code _____

Dear Mayor _____:

I am a student at _____.

I have some ideas to help improve our community.

1. _____

_____

_____

_____

2. _____

_____

_____

_____

I think these ideas are important. Please let me know
if I can do anything to help make these things happen.

Sincerely,

Name: _____

Name _____ Date _____

My State Symbols

1. What does your state flag look like? Draw it. Explain what the colors and symbols mean.

2. Draw and label your state bird.

3. Draw and label your state flower.

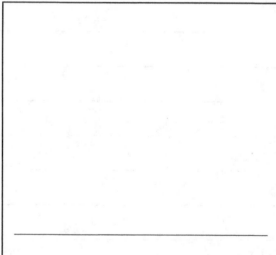

4. Draw and label your state tree.

5. List some other symbols of your state.

_____

_____

_____

_____

The case of *Little Pig and Mr. Wolf* is based on the story of "The Three Little Pigs."

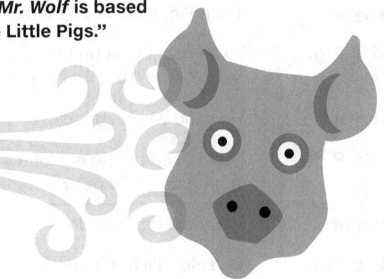

The Parts
- Narrator
- Little Pig
- Mr. Wolf
- Mrs. Sheep
- Lawyer
- Judge

Director's Note:

The Big Bad Wolf is being tried in court for destruction of property.

Lawyer:	You are accused of breaking the law by blowing down a house.
Mr. Wolf:	I am not guilty. I did not do it on purpose.
Lawyer:	In your own words, tell us what happened.
Mr. Wolf:	I had a bad cough.
Lawyer:	How did the house collapse?
Mr. Wolf:	I coughed?
Little Pig:	Not true! He blew down my straw house on purpose!
Lawyer:	Objection, your honor. The pig is not on the stand!
Judge:	Quiet down, Little Pig. You will get your turn.
Lawyer:	Continue, Mr. Wolf.
Mr. Wolf:	I coughed. A big cough. I accidentally blew down the house.

Judge:	Let's hear what Little Pig has to say.
Lawyer:	Little Pig, what happened on the day in question?
Little Pig:	I was cooking soup for supper. The wolf came by and said, "Little Pig, Little Pig, let me come in."
Lawyer:	How did you respond?
Little Pig:	I said, "Not by the hair of my chinny chin chin." I was frightened. I did not want the wolf in my house.
Lawyer:	What did the wolf do next?
Little Pig:	He said, "I'll huff and I'll puff, and I'll blow your house in." Then he blew my house down. I have witnesses—my neighbors, the sheep family.
Judge:	Call the witnesses.
Lawyer:	Mrs. Sheep, what did you witness?
Mrs. Sheep:	The wolf said to me, "Baa, baa black sheep, have you any wool?" I said, "No! Go away!" Then he went to Little Pig's house.
Lawyer:	What happened next?
Mrs. Sheep:	When Little Pig would not let Mr. Wolf in, the wolf blew down the house. All that was left was a pile of straw. My little ones ate it.
Little Pig:	They ate my house!
Mrs. Sheep:	They were hungry.
Mr. Wolf:	See! I didn't destroy the house. The sheep ate it.
Mrs. Sheep:	They wouldn't have eaten it if you hadn't blown it down first.
Narrator:	*What laws do you think were broken? Should someone go to jail? Who should rebuild the house? Share your ideas.*

Chapter 5

Citizenship and Civic Engagement

Objectives

- Identify the traits and roles of good citizens.
- Discuss the qualities and traits of good citizens demonstrated by famous Americans.
- Create a public service announcement to explain what makes an ideal citizen.

Quest Project-Based Learning: Being an Ideal Citizen				
	Description	**Duration**	**Materials**	**Participants**
STEP 1 Set the Stage	Read a blackline master as an introduction to the project.	15 minutes	**Blackline Master:** Quest Kick Off	Whole Class
STEP 2 Launch the Activities	Watch a video with background information.	15 minutes	**Video:** Volunteering: Mentor, Tutor, Friend **Leveled Readers:** Who Is Eleanor Roosevelt?; An American Hero: Eleanor Roosevelt; Eleanor Roosevelt: First Lady and Human Rights Leader	Whole Class
Activity 1 What Would You Do?	Resolve a scenario by demonstrating one of the traits of citizenship.	40 minutes	**Blackline Master:** What Would You Do?	Small Groups
Activity 2 Portrait of a Good Citizen	Create a good citizen illustration.	30 minutes	Drawing tools	Small Groups
Activity 3 Who Were Good Citizens?	Read and sort short biographies of well-known citizens.	35 minutes	**Blackline Master:** American Heroes scissors, glue	Small Groups
Activity 4 Choosing a Hero	Create a song or poem about a hero.	40 minutes	Research materials	Small Groups
Activity 5 ELL Public Service Announcement Script	Create a script for a public service announcement.	45 minutes	**Blackline Master:** Public Service Announcement Script	Individuals

STEP 3 Complete the Quest Prepare for the PSA	Prepare to deliver a public service announcement.	30 minutes	PSA Scripts (from Activity 5)	Whole Class
Deliver the PSA	Present a public service announcement to audience members.	30 minutes	PSA Scripts (from Activity 5)	Whole Class
Answer the **Compelling** **Question**	Discuss the compelling question.	20 minutes	**Student Activity Mat:** 4B Quest	Whole Class

Quick Activities

	Description	Duration	Materials	Participants
Citizenship Over Time	Discuss how the idea of citizenship has changed across time.	25 minutes	**Blackline Master:** Citizenship Over Time	Whole Class
Medal of Citizenship ELL	Create and design a medal of citizenship to award to a local hero.	35 minutes	**Blackline Master:** Medal of Citizenship **Student Activity Mat:** 4A Who, What, Where in the United States?	Partners, Individuals
How Can I Help My Community?	Decide on a plan to help the local community.	20 minutes		Whole Class
Biography Trading Cards	Create a trading card to highlight how a national or local hero shows the traits of an ideal citizen.	30 minutes	**Blackline Master:** Biography Trading Card	Individuals
Readers Theater: Johnny Appleseed	Read and act out a script about Johnny Appleseed.	20 minutes	**Blackline Master:** Johnny Appleseed	Whole Class

Project-Based Learning: Being an Ideal Citizen

Compelling Question

What is an ideal citizen?

Welcome to Quest 5, Being an Ideal Citizen. Students will explore and understand five traits of citizenship: honesty, compassion, respect, responsibility, and courage. Students will then prepare and present a public service announcement to explain the traits of an ideal citizen. After completing these activities, students will be able to discuss the compelling question at the end of this inquiry.

Objectives

- Identify the traits and roles of good citizens.
- Discuss the qualities and traits of good citizens demonstrated by famous Americans.
- Create a public service announcement to explain what makes an ideal citizen.

STEP 1 Set the Stage (15) minutes

Begin the Quest by distributing the blackline master **Quest Kick Off.** It will bring the world of the Quest to life, introducing a story to interest students and a mission to motivate them.

Story

The local news channel has asked each student to prepare a public service announcement that explains what it means to be an ideal citizen. The announcement will help to spread ideas of what it takes to be a good citizen.

···

Mission

Create a public service announcement to teach others about what makes an ideal citizen. A public service announcement is a message created in order to change a group's behavior or way of thinking.

STEP 2 Launch the Activities

The following five activities will help students prepare for their presentations delivering public service announcements about what it means to be an ideal citizen. Note that all five can be done independently of the larger Quest.

Begin by showing the chapter video, Volunteering: Mentor, Tutor, Friend, which shows how someone can be a good citizen in a community. You may also assign the appropriate leveled reader for this chapter.

Divide students into small groups that will remain consistent for all the activities.

Activity 1 What Would You Do? (40) minutes

Materials: Blackline Master: What Would You Do?

In this activity, small groups solve a dilemma using traits of citizenship.

Place the following traits into a chart for students:

- Honesty: when you speak the truth

- Compassion: caring about other people

- Respect: how you treat others

- Responsibility: having the job of taking care of something, someone, or yourself

- Courage: doing the right thing even when it is hard

Distribute the blackline master **What Would You Do?,** which lists five different scenarios. Assign each group one scenario.

Give groups time to read through and decide how to solve the scenario. Then allow groups to present their scenarios to the class, the solutions they chose, and the traits of citizenship being applied. Then ask the class, "How do these traits help us to participate in our classroom? In our community?"

Activity 2 Portrait of a Good Citizen (30) minutes

Students create a good citizen illustration.

Remind students of the five traits of citizenship discussed in Activity 1.

Share a small anecdote of a good citizen from the local community. Instruct students to draw an illustration showing what is considered being a "good citizen." Ask students to present and explain their illustrations. Encourage them to identify at least one of the five traits of citizenship in their explanations.

Activity 3   Who Were Good Citizens? minutes

Materials: Blackline Master: American Heroes, five-column chart, scissors, glue

Small groups work to sort biographies into the five traits of citizenship categories.

Have students create their own five-column charts. Have them add "Honesty" in the first column, "Compassion" in the second column, "Respect" in the third column, "Responsibility" in the fourth column, and "Courage" in the fifth column.

Distribute the blackline master **American Heroes.** Read through the first biography with students. Model how to decide that Abraham Lincoln demonstrates the trait of honesty. Instruct students to cut out the picture of Abraham Lincoln, along with his name, and glue it into the honesty column on the chart.

Instruct students to continue reading and sorting the descriptions with a partner. Tell students that if the person fits in more than one category, they can write the name of the person into the additional columns.

After all the pictures have been sorted, ask the class to discuss placement and to notice which qualities seem to appear most often.

Activity 4   Choosing a Hero minutes

Materials: Research materials

Small groups create a song or poem about a national or local hero.

Display a list of national and local heroes. Divide students into groups and have each group select a hero. Provide each group with background information about the hero.

Write the following questions on the board:

- What citizenship quality did the hero demonstrate?

- What did the hero risk when he or she performed his or her service?

Instruct students to use the biographies provided in Activity 3 and additional research to answer the questions. Tell each group to write a song or poem about their hero to present to the class.

After every small group has presented, ask students to discuss each of the qualities of citizenship that were found in each poem or song.

Activity 5 | Public Service Announcement Script ⏱ 45 minutes

Materials: Blackline Master: Public Service Announcement Script

Tell students that they will be preparing their scripts for a public service announcement about what it takes to be an ideal citizen. Explain that a public service announcement (PSA) is a message created in order to change a group's behavior or way of thinking. Use one of the following links to discuss an example of a PSA: https://www.ready.gov/psa-multimedia, https://www.psacentral.org/campaigns.

Distribute the blackline master **Public Service Announcement Script.** Inform students that their announcement should be about 20–30 seconds long. Explain that in order to convince people to listen to their message they should:

- Know the goal: to share what it takes to be an ideal citizen

- Have a clear message:

  - Think of words that convey your message.

  - Think of a catchy slogan or phrase (suggest using lines from the poem in Activity 4).

  - What are your facts? How can you share these dramatically?

Give students time to work on the script outline. Work with students while they practice reading and delivering their PSAs using their outlines. You may wish to help students produce videos in which the PSAs are performed.

....

🔵 Support for English Language Learners

Speaking Students will practice the skill of sharing ideas during a conversation to add to the conversation and to keep it going. They will focus on listening actively and sharing what they notice, what they think, and an idea they have during the conversation.

Entering: Have students draw and label an illustration of a person demonstrating good citizenship.

Emerging: Have students draw an illustration of a person demonstrating good citizenship. Then have the students complete the following sentence frame based on their illustrations: _____ *shows good citizenship.*

Developing: Show students a picture of a person demonstrating good citizenship. Pair students with partners. Instruct partners to state, in a few words, one thing they notice in the picture. Then have the student ask the partner the question, "What do you notice?"

Expanding: Have students complete the Developing activity. Instruct students to listen actively and to build on the conversation by stating one idea they have from what they noticed. For example, "I noticed the woman holding the door open for the child."

Bridging: Have students complete the Developing activity. Instruct students to build onto the conversation, actively listening to their partner and stating ideas they have from what they noticed. Also ask each student to state which trait of citizenship a character from the visual aid is displaying.

STEP 3 Complete the *Quest*

Part 1 Prepare for the PSA (30) minutes

Materials: PSA Scripts (from Activity 5)

Prepare students for the presentations by discussing the traits of an ideal citizen. Ask students to share examples from national and local heroes to support their thinking about what it takes to be an ideal citizen. Tell students to listen closely to the public service announcements of their peers.

Part 2 Deliver the PSA (30) minutes

Depending on the options you gave for the presentation, you will set up the room accordingly.

Audio Presentation: If you prerecord students, then set up the room so students can hear the prerecorded messages as if listening to the radio. Have each group take turns listening to each presentation. Allow groups to quietly share their thoughts after each PSA.

Live Presentation: If you have students read their scripts to the class, other classes, administration, and parents, then you may opt to set up the classroom like it is a press conference room with a podium and chairs. Allow students to step up to the podium to deliver their messages and sit down directly after.

Video Presentation: If you video record students doing their PSAs, then set up the room so students can hear and see the videos. You may decide to spend 30 seconds after each PSA allowing students to offer compliments.

Once all students have shared their PSAs, ask the class again to describe the traits of an ideal citizen. Make sure students are giving examples from one another's PSAs in their responses. Congratulate the class on completing the Quest.

Part 3 Compelling Question (20) minutes

After the students present, encourage them to reflect on what they learned. As a class, discuss the compelling question for this Quest: "What is an ideal citizen?"

Students have learned and discussed five different traits of good citizenship: honesty, compassion, respect, responsibility, and courage. Students have identified the traits in action by studying the words and lives of many national and local heroes. They should use what they learned to answer the compelling question.

Have students use Student Activity Mat 4B Quest to reflect on the Quest Activities.

Quest Kick Off

Name _____ Date _____

Being an Ideal Citizen

The local news station wants to make an announcement to spread ideas of what it takes to be a good citizen. They've asked you to prepare a public service announcement to explain to the public how they can be ideal citizens.

Your Mission
Create a public service announcement to teach others about what makes an ideal citizen. A public service announcement is a message created in order to change a group's behavior or way of thinking.

To create and present your public service announcement:

Activity 1 **What Would You Do?:** Resolve a scenario using a citizenship trait.

Activity 2 **Portrait of a Good Citizen:** Create a good citizen illustration.

Activity 3 **Who Were Good Citizens?:** Sort biographies into traits of citizenship categories.

Activity 4 **Choosing a Hero:** Create a song or poem about a national or local hero.

Activity 5 **Public Service Announcement Script:** Write a script for the public service announcement.

Complete Your Quest

Create and present your public service announcement.

Name _____ Date _____

What Would You Do?

> Discuss one of the following scenarios with your group and decide what to do. Use at least one of these traits in your decision: honesty, compassion, respect, responsibility, courage.

Scenario 1: Missing Homework

You had a late soccer practice, and you were too tired to complete your math homework. You decided you would do it first thing in the morning, but you woke up late and got to school just as class was starting. Your teacher is collecting everyone's math homework for a grade.

What would you do? _____

Scenario 2: Stay Up Late?

Your parents are attending a community group meeting, and they won't be home until after your bedtime. You know that bedtime CANNOT be changed on a school night, but your baby sitter doesn't know when your bedtime is. You notice that your parents' note explaining the nightly routine has slipped under the kitchen counter. Your bedtime is written on your note, and the baby sitter will get in trouble if you go to bed late.

What would you do? _____

Scenario 3: Cutting in Line

Everyone in town is excited that the new smoothie shop has finally opened. There is a line around the block, and you will have to wait at least 45 minutes. You recognize someone from your grade at the front of the line.

What would you do? _____

Scenario 4: Breaking a Vase

Your mom ALWAYS tells you to play ball outside because she doesn't want anything broken in the house. You are just throwing the ball up and down to break in your new mitt, so you don't think it's a big deal to play inside. You throw the ball too hard, and it bounces on the coffee table and breaks your mom's vase. You know she is going to be very mad at you.

What would you do? _____

Scenario 5: The Bully

After school, you always go to the community park with your friends. One day, a bully decides to pick on your friend. He takes his backpack and puts it up high, so your friend can't reach it.

What would you do? _____

American Heroes

Read through the biographies and decide which trait
of citizenship each person shows.

Abraham Lincoln (1809–1865) 	• He worked as a respectable store clerk in Illinois. • As president, he led the nation through the Civil War, which resulted in the end of slavery in the United States. • Lincoln would tell people directly what he did or did not appreciate about them.
Anne Hutchinson (1591–1643) 	• Anne Hutchinson moved from England to Boston in the 1600s to practice her religion freely. • She believed in freedom of thought and wanted to worship as she pleased instead of following the strict laws of the Puritans. • Forced to leave Boston because of her religious beliefs, she moved to an area that became the state of Rhode Island. She continued to practice and speak out about her beliefs.
Benjamin Franklin (1706–1790) 	• Franklin was an author, scientist, politician, printer, inventor, and diplomat. • He was one of the Founding Fathers of the United States of America. • By 1781, Franklin freed his slaves and spoke out against the system of slavery. • He believed in "virtues," such as justice (fairness) and sincerity (honesty).

Thomas Jefferson (1743–1826) 	• He had a passion for learning and spent up to 14 hours per day studying. • He was the author of the Declaration of Independence, for which the British could have arrested him. • He was the third U.S. president.
Harriet Tubman (c. 1820–1913) 	• She was a slave but escaped to freedom. • She helped free hundreds of enslaved African Americans in the Underground Railroad by returning to the South and leading them north to freedom. Each journey risked her life. • She worked as a cook, nurse, scout, and spy for the Union Army during the Civil War. • She was also a women's rights activist.
Clara Barton (1821–1912) 	• She worked as a battlefield nurse during the Civil War, risking her life to bring soldiers medicine and supplies. • She started the Red Cross organization to care for people who are victims of floods and other natural disasters.
Eleanor Roosevelt (1884–1962) 	• She was the First Lady from 1933–1945. • She fought for human rights all over the world, especially for women, children, and African Americans. • She helped create the Universal Declaration of Human Rights, which stated that every person in the world had human rights.

Activity 5

Public Service Announcement Script

Use the spaces in the chart to plan your script. Fill in the blanks to begin writing your script.

	Write Your Notes:
Goal: Write the message you want the audience to receive.	
Reasons: List reasons for being an ideal citizen.	
Facts: List facts to support the reasons.	

Do you know what it takes to be an ideal citizen?
[Insert message here.]

_____

It is important to be an ideal citizen because [Insert two reasons here.]

_____

Did you know [Insert fact to support reason here.]

_____

Let's encourage people to become ideal citizens.
[Insert catchy phrase or song here.]

_____

Quick Activities

Citizenship Over Time

Whole Class 25 minutes

Materials: Blackline Master: Citizenship Over Time

Students discuss how the idea of citizenship has changed over time.

Work with students to think about what it means to be a good citizen today. Reference the five traits of citizenship discussed earlier: honesty, compassion, respect, responsibility, and courage. (See Quest Activity 1 for more details.)

Distribute the blackline master **Citizenship Over Time.** Discuss the images and information with students. Then have them answer the questions.

As a class, create a Venn diagram to compare and contrast the colonial child's viewpoint to the industrial laborer child's viewpoint. Ask, "How has the idea of an ideal citizen changed since then?"

Medal of Citizenship

Materials: Blackline Master: Medal of Citizenship

Students create and design a medal of citizenship to award to a local hero.

If desired, read aloud *Separate Is Never Equal: Sylvia Mendez and Her Family's Fight for Desegregation* by Duncan Tonatiuh. Lead the class in a conversation about the courage that Sylvia Mendez and her family displayed.

Ask students to work in pairs to research other local heroes. (Refer to local newspapers for names of individuals for the activity.) Have students use Student Activity Mat 4A Who, What, Where in the United States? to make notes about the individuals they research. After students have completed their research, instruct them to select one inspirational hero to use as they complete the activity.

Distribute the blackline master **Medal of Citizenship.** Then instruct students to design a medal of citizenship to award to the local hero. Remind students to decorate the medal appropriately by illustrating the traits of citizenship. Tell students they must prepare a few words explaining why the hero deserves the medal.

....

🄴🄻🄻 Support for English Language Learners

Speaking Review with students how to exchange information and ideas in a conversation through oral collaborative discussions. Remind students that using details can strengthen and improve their conversations. Review turn-taking and how to ask relevant questions by staying on topic.

Entering: Instruct students to label their blackline master with one word that describes an ideal citizen. State the word aloud and have the student repeat the word.

Emerging: Have students choose at least one characteristic of an ideal citizen that is exhibited by the hero chosen. Then have students complete the following sentence frames: *I chose _____ because he/she is an ideal citizen. He/she shows _____.*

Developing: Organize students into pairs. Encourage one partner to name one reason why their selected hero is an ideal citizen. Have the other partner ask a yes or no question about the hero. Provide examples, if needed: "Does your hero give back to others?" "Do other people in the community think this person is a hero?" Then switch roles.

Expanding: Organize students into pairs. Encourage one partner to name one reason why their selected hero is an ideal citizen. Have the other partner ask a question about which trait of citizenship best describes the hero. Then switch roles.

Bridging: Organize students into pairs. Instruct students to have a conversation about how local heroes give back to their communities. Encourage students to give some examples of different heroes who have helped change the community. Ensure students are asking and answering questions and following turn-taking rules appropriately. Provide some questions and sentence frames, such as: *Who is another ideal citizen in our community? I think (insert name) is an ideal citizen because _____.*

How Can I Help My Community?

Whole Class (20) **minutes**

Students formulate a plan for helping their community.

Create a list of problems in the local community (such as homelessness, high poverty, lack of food and clothing, or lack of recycling). As a class, decide on a problem to focus on, and brainstorm class service projects (such as holding a food/clothing drive, sponsoring an Adopt-a-Highway program, creating awareness posters, volunteering at a shelter, or creating public service announcement videos that can air on a local news station).

After the brainstorming session, commit class time or time outside of class to engage in the service-learning project related to the issue.

Finally, ask students, "How do you help your community on a regular basis?"

Biography Trading Cards

Individuals (30) **minutes**

Materials: Blackline Master: Biography Trading Card

Students create a trading card to highlight the traits of an ideal citizen shown by a hero.

Ask students to select an international or local hero. The person selected must demonstrate one of the traits of citizenship: honesty, compassion, respect, responsibility, or courage. Here is a list of suggested heroes:

Anne Hutchinson	Harriet Tubman	Nelson Mandela	Anne Frank
Ben Franklin	Clara Barton	Mahatma Gandhi	Thomas Paine
Thomas Jefferson	Eleanor Roosevelt	Helen Keller	Amelia Earhart
Abraham Lincoln	Martin Luther King Jr.	Jackie Robinson	Paul Revere
Frederick Douglass	César Chávez	Marie Curie	Ruby Bridges

Distribute the blackline master **Biography Trading Card.** Instruct students to research basic information about their selected heroes. Finally, allow students to share or trade cards.

Name _____ Date _____

Citizenship Over Time

Study the pictures and information. Then answer the questions in the right column.

Colonial America, 1600s and 1700s

- People worked hard as a family to grow food to eat and sell.
- The closest neighbor or farm was miles away.
- Children were educated at home by their mothers.
- Some families attended church on Sunday where they interacted with other families.

What do you think being a good citizen meant to this child?

_____
_____
_____
_____
_____
_____

Child Labor, Late 1800s

- Children as young as five would work many hours a day for very low wages.
- Working children had no time to play or go to school and little time to sleep.

What do you think being a good citizen meant to this child?

_____
_____
_____
_____

Medal of Citizenship

Design a medal of citizenship.

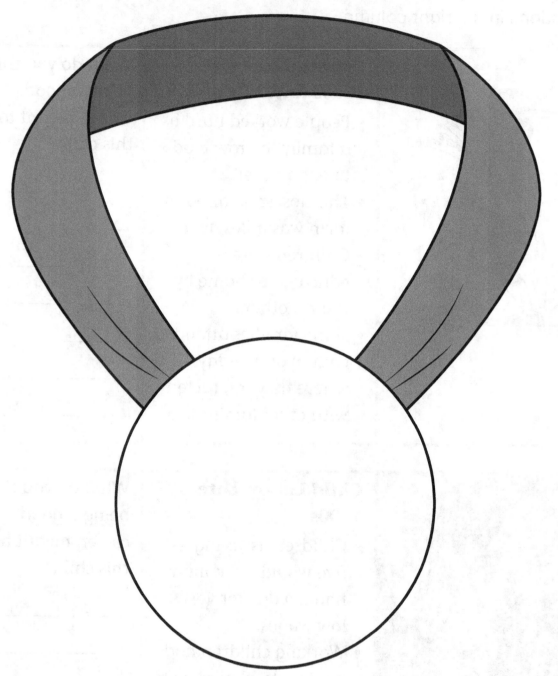

Why does the hero deserve this medal?

_____

_____

Biography Trading Card

Fill out the trading card with information about one national
or local hero who shows the traits of good citizenship.

HERO

Name:

THE FACTS

Job

_____

IMPACT Made on Others

Other Facts

This story is about an encounter Johnny Appleseed had with another man, Thomas, and a snake while walking the land spreading his seeds. This story is an example of a legend.

The Parts

- **Narrator**
- **Johnny**
- **Thomas**

Director's Notes:

Narrator: Johnny Appleseed was a real person who planted apples. Over time, the story of Johnny Appleseed has turned into a legend, which is a traditional story with some made-up details.

John Chapman, who is known as Johnny Appleseed, was one of twelve children who grew up in Massachusetts. One day, he left his home to make a difference in the world by sharing and spreading his apple seeds. His love of nature and animals was seen wherever he traveled. He traveled around barefoot! His clothes were made from flour sacks, and his hat was a tin pot that he used to cook his meals. He didn't carry or use weapons. All he had with him was a bag filled with apple seeds from the cider mill back home.

Johnny walks onstage, humming a tune and acting as though planting seeds. At center stage he bumps into Thomas.

Thomas:	Excuse me. What are you doing on my land?
Johnny:	Sorry, sir. I was just planting some apple seeds. I didn't know this was your land.
Thomas: *pointing at the ground*	Watch out! It's a rattlesnake!

Narrator: Johnny is face to face with the rattlesnake. The snake bares its fangs at Johnny and hisses. It bites Johnny's foot! But Johnny's feet are so thick from walking around barefoot that the snake can't break through his skin. The snake starts to back away, but Johnny picks it up.

Johnny:
bending down

Don't be afraid, little snake. We are all here to work together on this land. Thomas and his family don't want to hurt you either. Why don't you stay hidden over yonder in the forest and leave everyone alone over here?

Thomas: I've never seen anything like that before in my life. That snake seemed to have listened to you. Look at it slithering away to the forest. How did you do that? You must have magical powers!

Johnny: I just assured him that we didn't mean him any harm. People and animals can learn to get along. Why, just the other day, I slept the whole night with a bear and her cub in a hollowed-out tree log.

Thomas: That sure is amazing. Why do you travel around these parts with apple seeds anyway?

Johnny: I want to make my mark on the world and make it a better place. What better way than spreading the delicious growth of apples from my family's orchards and by bringing peace along the way.

Thomas: You are a respectable, responsible young man. Sure wish there were more people like you in this world. Good day to you.

Johnny:
tips his tin hat and continues on his way

Good day to you, too.

Chapter 6 A Growing Nation

Objectives

- Identify and describe how communities change over time.
- Describe important people, places, and events in U.S. history.
- Explain why people immigrate to new lands.

- Analyze how innovations in transportation, communication, ideas, and technology influenced the United States.
- Write a news report that tells about what life was like in the past.

Quest Document-Based Writing: Presenting a News Report

	Description	Duration	Materials	Participants
STEP 1 Set the Stage	Read a blackline master as an introduction to the project.	15 minutes	**Blackline Master:** Quest Kick Off	Whole Class
STEP 2 Launch the Activities	Watch a video with background information.	5 minutes	**Leveled Readers:** New Beginnings; Early America; Starting Out **Video:** National Inventors Hall of Fame	Whole Class
Activity 1 Analyzing a Timeline	Summarize a historical event.	45 minutes	**Blackline Master:** Timeline of U.S. History index cards	Individuals
Activity 2 Let's Investigate	Form questions about important people and events in U.S. history.	45 minutes	**Blackline Master:** People in U.S. History	Individuals
Activity 3 Finding Answers	Conduct research to answer the questions from Activity 2.	45 minutes	Questions from Activity 2, research tools	Small Groups
Activity 4 Who? What? Where? When?	Record answers to questions about a specific topic.	45 minutes	**Student Activity Mat 4A:** Who, What, Where in the United States?	Small Groups
STEP 3 ELL Complete the Quest Prepare a News Report	Prepare a news report on a specific topic.	30 minutes	**Blackline Master:** News Report Checklist	Small Groups
Deliver a News Report	Deliver a news report as an audio or video report, or a live newscast.	45 minutes		Small Groups
Answer the **Compelling Question**	Reflect on life in the past in the United States to answer the compelling question.	15 minutes		Whole Class

Quick Activities

	Description	Duration	Materials	Participants
Our Community ⓔ	Add local stories to the class timeline.	30 minutes	**Student Activity Mat 3B:** Time and Place, index cards	Small Groups
What's in a Name?	Analyze where state and city names came from.	30 minutes	**Blackline Master:** Place Names	Whole Class
Changes Over Time	Create a class book about how their community has changed over time.	30 minutes	**Blackline Master:** Recording Sheet	Small Groups
Readers Theater: A New Life in America	Perform a script about an immigrant in America.	30 minutes	**Blackline Master:** A New Life in America	Whole Class

Document-Based Writing: Presenting a News Report

Compelling Question Why was life in the past difficult?

Welcome to Quest 6, Presenting a News Report. In this Quest, your students will research and write a television script about life in the United States long ago. By researching and writing about a topic they are interested in, they will gain insight to help answer the compelling question at the end of this inquiry.

Objectives

• Identify and describe how communities change over time.
• Describe important people, places, and events in U.S. history.
• Explain why people immigrate to new lands.
• Analyze how innovations in transportation, communication, ideas, and technology influenced the United States.
• Write a news report that tells about what life was like in the past.

STEP 1 Set the Stage (15) minutes

Begin the Quest by distributing the blackline master **Quest Kick Off.** It will bring the world of the Quest to life, introducing a story to interest students and a mission to motivate them.

Story

A news station wants to produce a weekly feature about life in the United States long ago. They need students to research and write the script for one report, and then present their report on the air.

....

Mission

Students must research and write the script for one episode. They can choose from the following topics: travel, immigration, settlement, communication, or new ideas. After they have completed their scripts, they must deliver their report on the news.

STEP 2 Launch the Activities

The following four activities will help students prepare for their news report by researching and gathering information about a specific time period in history. Note that all four can be done independently of the larger Quest.

Begin by showing the chapter video National Inventors Hall of Fame, which will provide some background about inventions in U.S. history. You may also assign the appropriate Leveled Reader for this chapter.

Then divide students into small groups that will remain consistent for all the activities.

Activity 1 Analyzing a Timeline (45) minutes

Materials: Blackline Master: Timeline of U.S. History, index cards

Distribute the blackline master **Timeline of U.S. History.** Make sure students understand that this timeline only gives a glimpse into the dense history of the United States. There are many other important events that are not on this timeline. Read aloud the dates and events with students. Stop to discuss any questions or comments students might have as they read.

Ask students to select an event from the timeline that they find interesting or want to know more about. Make sure students have different events. Give students time and resources to research more about the event.

Distribute index cards to each student. Instruct them to draw an illustration of the event on one side of the card with the date. Have them write a brief explanation of the event on the other side of the card.

Finally, ask students to share their events in chronological order. Display each card on a hanging class timeline, using, for example, a clothesline strung across the room.

Activity 2 Let's Investigate . . . (45) minutes

Materials: Blackline Master: People in U.S. History

If possible, read aloud from *Sitting Bull: Lakota Warrior and Defender of His People* by S.D. Nelson, or *28 Days: Moments in Black History That Changed the World* by Charles R. Smith Jr.

Discuss with students what it means to be an investigative reporter. Say something similar to "Investigative reporting is a form of gathering facts and information. Most investigative reporters have an idea about what they want to say, or they have questions they want answered before reporting."

Distribute the blackline master **People in U.S. History.** Inform students that they will practice reading and forming questions about important places, people, groups, or events from earlier eras. Read through the informative paragraphs as a class.

Then give students time to write five to six questions about the place, time, and topic they have chosen. They will research and answer these questions during Activity 3.

Activity 3 — Finding Answers 45 minutes

Materials: Questions from Activity 2, research tools

Inform students that the trick to investigative reporting is keeping the interest of the audience. A news report does not just list a string of facts. It needs to provide interesting facts with strong supporting details or interesting stories.

Tell students it's now time to conduct research to find answers to their questions from Activity 2. If possible, use the school's media specialist during this activity, so students can access a wide range of research tools. Give students time to conduct their research.

Instruct students to record answers to their questions from Activity 2 in complete sentences. Encourage students to write at least two to three sentences per question in order to gather enough information to use for the news script. If students find other interesting information they want to present, have them write that information, too.

Activity 4 — Who? What? Where? When? 45 minutes

Materials: Student Activity Mat 4A Who, What, Where in the United States?

Remind students that investigative reporting tries to capture what life was like for everyone. Distribute the Student Activity Mat 4A Who, What, Where in the United States? Write the following headings on the board: Who? What? Where? When? Instruct students to answer these questions in each of the four boxes on their Mat.

Then remind students of the topics they and others have researched: travel, immigration, settlement, communication, and new ideas.

Inform students that there will be more information for some of these topics than others. Instruct students to fill in facts about their topic for each category on the Activity Mat during their period. Allow students time to research if needed.

Ask students to share information about their selected topic. Encourage students to answer basic questions, such as:

• What was life like?

• What did houses look like?

• What food did the people eat?

• What kinds of jobs did most people have?

Discuss differences for each period and topic.

Part 1 Prepare a News Report ⏲ 30 minutes

Materials: Blackline Master: News Report Checklist

Display the presentation rubric for the class. Review all the criteria and allow students to comment or ask questions.

Show students a clip from PBS, *Sixty Minutes*, or another investigative news show. Ask students what they noticed about news reporting.

Distribute the blackline master **News Report Checklist.** Discuss the elements of a news report by reading through the checklist.

Give students time to write their news scripts. Then provide students with the following presentation options:

- **An Audio News Report.** Record students reading their news story, as if they are calling in to a live news show. Play the recording for the class.

- **A Video Production.** Record students delivering their news story and air as part of a school or district news program.

- **Live Report.** Students deliver their news story live in front of the class.

Use the Informative/Explanatory Writing rubric to assess the news scripts.

ⓔⓛⓛ Support for English Language Learners

Speaking Have students review how to prepare for an oral presentation by practicing with the scripts they wrote. Remind students that they should try to make eye contact and look around the room when presenting.

Entering: Encourage students to draw a picture that enhances their topic. Have them label the picture and practice saying the label aloud and describing what it shows.

Emerging: Have students choose one sentence frame to describe their topic:
People traveled by _____. People came to the United States from _____. People settled in _____. People communicated by _____. A new idea was _____.
Then, have pairs practice saying their sentences to each other.

Developing: Ask students to write two facts about their topic. Have students choose one or more sentence starter to use both of their facts:
People traveled . . . . People came to the United States from . . . . People settled in . . . . People communicated by . . . . Some new ideas of the time were . . . .
Then, have pairs practice saying their sentences to each other.

Expanding: Ask students to write three sentences about their topic. Give students time to individually practice saying their sentences aloud. Then have student pairs deliver their sentences to each other.

Bridging: Ask students to write three to four facts about their topic. Give students time to put the facts together into complete sentences that flow logically from one idea to the next. Then have student pairs practice their oral presentations with each other.

Part 2 Deliver a News Report minutes

Materials: Completed News Report Scripts

Students will present their news report in one of three forms:

• Play the audio news report

• Play the video news report

• Read their news report live in front of the class

Part 3 Answer the Compelling Question ⏱ 15 minutes

After students present their news stories, encourage them to reflect on what they learned. As a class, discuss the compelling question for this Quest "Why was life in the past difficult?"

Students have learned about people, places, ways to travel, immigration, settlement, communication, and new ideas in the United States in the past, focusing on challenges people faced. They should use what they learned to answer the compelling question.

Presenting a News Report

A news station wants to produce a weekly feature about life in the United States long ago. They need you to research and write the script for one report, and then present your report on the air.

Your Mission

Your mission is to research and write the script for one episode. You can choose from the following topics: travel, immigration, settlement, communication, or new ideas. After you have completed your script, you must deliver your report on the air.

To make and present your television script, work with your team to do the following:

Activity 1 | **Analyzing a Timeline:** Illustrate, research, and summarize one event.

Activity 2 | **Let's Investigate . . . :** Write questions about important places, people, groups, or events from earlier eras.

Activity 3 | **Finding Answers:** Conduct research to answer your questions from Activity 2.

Activity 4 | **Who? What? Where? When?:** Record information about a specific topic.

Complete Your Quest

Present your news report as a recorded audio production, a video, or a live broadcast.

Timeline of U.S. History

1500s Europeans begin to settle in North America.

1775 The Revolutionary War begins.

1775 Daniel Boone widens the Cumberland Gap.

1783 The United States wins independence from Great Britain.

1796 Edward Jenner develops the smallpox vaccine.

1804 Lewis and Clark begin to explore the land west of the Mississippi.

1813 Davy Crockett explores Tennessee.

1825 The Erie Canal connects the Great Lakes to New York City.

1831 Cyrus Hall McCormick invents the reaper.

1832 Samuel Morse develops the telegraph.

1838 Frederick Douglass escapes from slavery and begins speaking out.

1840s It takes six months to travel by covered wagon to Oregon.

1848 Gold is discovered in California.

1849–1859 Harriet Tubman helps enslaved people escape.

mid-1800s Thousands of immigrants from Europe and Asia arrive in the United States.

1860 The Pony Express begins.

1861 The Civil War begins.

1862 The Homestead Act encourages people to move West.

1863–1869 The Transcontinental Railroad is built.

1865 The Civil War ends.

1870s Sitting Bull leads his people during resistance to U.S. government policies.

1876 Alexander Graham Bell invents the telephone.

1879 Thomas Edison invents a light bulb.

1882 The U.S. government passes the Chinese Exclusion Act.

1901 The first radio message is sent across the Atlantic.

1903 The Wright brothers fly a plane for 12 seconds.

1903 Henry Ford opens a business that builds and sells cars.

1904 Mary McLeod Bethune opens a school for African American girls.

1939 The television is introduced to large numbers of people.

1950s Jonas Salk develops the polio vaccine.

1954 The U.S. Supreme Court rules that school segregation is not legal.

1956 An interstate highway system is begun.

1964 A new law makes it illegal to discriminate in the workplace.

1976 Steve Jobs starts Apple Computer in his family's garage.

People in U.S. History

Sitting Bull

Sitting Bull (*c.* 1831–1890) led Sioux groups in their struggle for survival on the Great Plains. He did not want to live on a reservation. Gold was discovered in South Dakota in 1874. Soon after, there was conflict with U.S. authorities. The Great Sioux wars of the 1870s ended in 1876 at Battle of the Little Bighorn. There Sitting Bull and Sioux groups defeated U.S. troops.

Several years later with his people starving, Sitting Bull surrendered and was forced to live on a reservation. In 1890, Sitting Bull was shot and killed by U.S. and Indian agents. They were afraid that Sitting Bull would lead a movement to restore the Sioux way of life.

Harriet Tubman

Harriet Tubman was born in Maryland in 1820. She was enslaved. In 1849, she escaped north to freedom. But she kept returning south to help others escape. She guided her parents, family members, and others to freedom. She was the most famous "conductor" on the Underground Railroad—a secret network of houses where people fleeing could rest. She also helped the Union Army during the Civil War. She was the first woman to lead an armed raid. The raid freed more than 700 enslaved people in South Carolina.

After the Civil War ended, Tubman helped former enslaved African Americans and the elderly.

What do you most admire about Sitting Bull or Harriet Tubman?

_____

_____

_____

_____

The Wright Brothers

The brothers Wilbur and Orville Wright built and repaired bicycles in Dayton, Ohio. They decided to build an airplane. But there were no engines light enough and powerful enough for their plane. They had to build the engine, too.

On December 17, 1903, Orville flew the plane in Kitty Hawk, South Carolina. The first flight lasted 12 seconds. The brothers made improvements to their plane. By 1905, they were flying for 30 minutes at a time. In 1909, the brothers opened the Wright Company to build airplanes.

Steve Jobs

Steve Jobs (1955–2011) was born in San Francisco, California, in 1955. In 1976, Jobs and a partner started Apple Computer in the garage of Steve's parents. To fund the company, Jobs sold his car. His partner sold his calculator.

Jobs and his partner changed the computer industry. They made machines smaller, cheaper, and easier to use. Apple introduced products, such as the iPhone, that other companies quickly copied.

What do you most admire about the Wright Brothers or Steve Jobs?

_____

_____

_____

_____

_____

_____

_____

Name _____ Date _____

News Report Checklist

Topic: _____

Main Idea: _____

Facts

Who? _____

What? _____

Where? _____

When? _____

Why? _____

How? _____

Headline: _____

Topic Sentence: _____

Conclusion: _____

_____

_____

Organize your ideas in a way that makes
sense. Use only the most important facts
that support your main idea. Think of a good
conclusion that briefly summarizes what you
have written in a sentence or two.

Quick Activities

Our Community

Materials: Student Activity Mat 3B Time and Place, Leveled Readers or other books about newcomers, index cards

In this activity, the class adds to the class timeline from Quest Activity 1 by including stories from their family history, or stories they have read about real local people.

You may want to read aloud *Migrant: The Journey of a Mexican Worker* by José Manuel Mateo, *Fiona's Lace* by Patricia Polacco, or *I'm New Here* by Anne Sibley O'Brien.

Engage students in a discussion about how or why their families moved to their current home and community. Invite each student to use Student Activity Mat 3B Time and Place to organize their own family timelines. Then distribute an index card to each student. Instruct students to draw an illustration of their story on one side. On the other side, have students write an explanation of what the illustration shows.

As students share their stories, add their index cards to the class timeline created in Quest Activity 1.

ELL Support for English Language Learners

Speaking Review with students how to exchange information and ideas in a conversation by asking questions. Remind students that using details can strengthen their explanations. Review how to take turns and how to ask questions that stay on topic.

Entering: Have the students write and practice saying the words *yes* and *no*. Then in pairs, have students ask each other simple questions that can be answered with *yes* or *no*.

Emerging: Have student pairs take turns answering and asking questions about their family using these sentence frames: *Did your family move? _____ (yes/no)*

When did your family move? (My family moved in _____.)

Developing: Divide students into pairs. Encourage one partner to say one reason their family moved to their house or community. Have the other student ask a yes-or-no question about the move. Provide examples, such as "How many moved?" "How old were you?" "Where did you move from?" Then switch roles.

Expanding: Divide students into pairs. Encourage one partner to tell a reason their family moved to their house or community using the sentence starter: My family moved here because . . . . Have the partner ask a question about when or why they moved. Then switch roles.

Bridging: Instruct student pairs to use details to discuss why people or their family came to their community. Make sure they both ask and answer questions and follow turn-taking rules appropriately.

What's in a Name?

Whole Class minutes

Materials: Blackline Master: Place Names

In this activity, students will discuss where place names come from.

Explain to students that names often come from the languages of the people who lived there or the history of the place. Ask students to read about the history of several places on the blackline master **Place Names.**

To extend the activity, provide students with a local neighborhood map. As a whole class, research the historical importance of a few local place names. If possible, visit the local historical society and have this research at hand before conducting the activity.

Changes Over Time

Small Groups (30) minutes

Materials: Blackline Master: Recording Sheet, Leveled Readers

In this activity, students create a book showing how their community has changed over time.

If possible, read aloud *The House on Maple Street* by Bonnie Pryor. The story demonstrates how one place changes over 300 years. Then show students photos or other primary source materials that show a street in your community. Use the local historical society to help gather and find materials for this activity.

Divide students into four small groups: Transportation, Immigrants, Events, and Jobs. Instruct each group to use the blackline master **Recording Sheet** to gather or draw pictures and record a few facts about their topic. Suggested time ranges: 1700s, 1800s, 1900s, and 2000s.

Assemble the **Recording Sheets** to make a class book about their community.

Readers Theater: A New Life in America

Materials: Blackline Master: A New Life in America

You may want to make available to students some stories about immigrants, such as *Migrant: The Journey of a Mexican Worker* by José Manuel Mateo, *Fiona's Lace* by Patricia Polacco, or *I'm New Here* by Anne Sibley O'Brien.

Distribute the blackline master **A New Life in America** to students. Explain that in the story, a family comes to the United States from another place.

Point out elements of a script, including the roles and dialogue. Explain that the director's notes give information about the play that isn't included in the dialogue.

Assign roles, and have students read aloud the script. Tell students they should try to use their voices to express emotion. For example, they can read faster or louder when a person is excited. They can speak quietly if a person is afraid. Remind students that listeners should pay close attention, and be respectful, polite, and interested.

Place Names

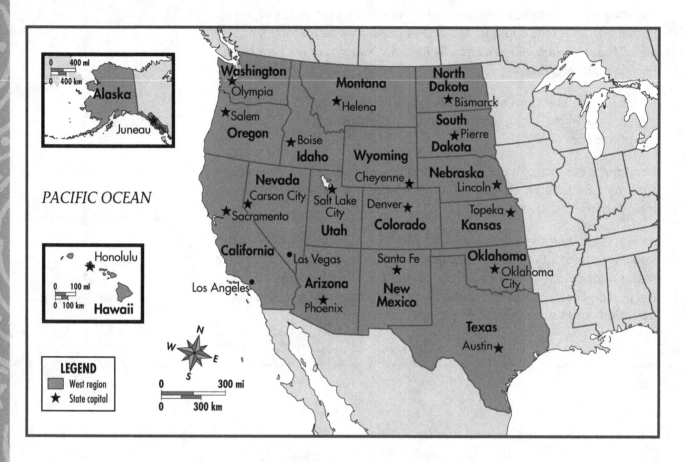

Many place names in the United States come from other languages and cultures and from people in history. Look at the places on the map. Then read to find out where some of the names came from.

- Alaska (from Aleut *alaxsxaq*, meaning "the place sea waves are directed at")
- Austin (named after Stephen F. Austin, the "Father of Texas," who brought 300 U.S. families to the region in 1835)
- Arizona (perhaps from Spanish *Arizonac*, probably from an O'odham [Piman] word meaning "having a little spring")
- Boise (from French *boisé* meaning "wooded")

- Cheyenne (a French version of the Dakota word *Sahi'yena*, a Dakotan name for the Cree people)
- Colorado (named for a river, called *Rio Colorado* in Spanish; *Colorado* means "reddish")
- Hawaii (from the Hawaiian word *Hawai'i* meaning "Place of the Gods")
- Honolulu (from Hawaiian meaning "sheltered harbor")
- Idaho (from Kiowa-Apache *idaahe* meaning "enemy")
- Juneau (named after French-Canadian miner Joe Juneau)
- Kansas (the French version of the Sioux word *Kansa*, the name of the people who lived there)
- Montana (from Spanish *montaña* meaning "mountain")
- Nebraska (perhaps from a Sioux name for the Platte River meaning "flat water")
- Nevada (named for the *Sierra Nevada* mountain range; *Nevada* is from the Spanish meaning "snowy")
- North Dakota (*Dakota* comes from a group of people from the Plains states; *Dakota* means "friendly")
- Oklahoma (from Choctaw; *Okla* means "nation" or "people")
- Oregon (probably from an Algonquian word)
- Pierre (named for the French fur trader Pierre Chouteau)
- Santa Fe (from Spanish meaning "holy faith")
- Seattle (named for *Seatlh*, a Salish chief friendly to settlers)
- Texas (from Spanish *Tejas*, the Spanish name for eastern Texas Indians called *Taysha*, which means "friends")
- Topeka (from Kansa meaning "a good place to dig potatoes")
- Utah (from Spanish *yuta*, the name of the people of the Great Basin, today called Utes)

Name _____ Date _____

Recording Sheet

Topic (Transportation, Immigrants, Events, Jobs): _____

Time Period (1700s, 1800s, 1900s, 2000s): _____

Fact 1: _____

_____

_____

_____

Fact 2: _____

_____

_____

_____

Fact 3: _____

_____

_____

_____

Images (sketch or describe):

A story about immigrants coming to the United States

The Parts

- **Narrator**
- **Mother**
- **Father**
- **Girl**
- **Boy**
- **Interpreter**

Director's Notes:

The play begins on a ship arriving in the United States from Europe. Thousands of people are packed on the decks of the ship at the end of the ten-day journey.

Father: We're here! I see the Statue of Liberty!

Boy: It's so beautiful Papa!

Girl: It is! I'm so happy to be in America at last.

Mother: We have been on this ship for ten days. It will be so nice to finally go ashore.

Narrator: The ship docks at Ellis Island, where immigrants are processed.

Girl:
looking at a number pinned to her coat
What are these numbers for?

Father: So officials can keep track of everyone. Stay together. We do not want to get separated.

Interpreter: I speak six languages. If you speak French, Spanish, Italian, Portuguese, German, or Dutch, come with me.

Narrator: The family follows the interpreter.

Interpreter: First, we need to walk past the doctor. He will see if you are healthy.

Narrator: The family stands in line. They watch as a man holding a piece of chalk inspects each person.

Interpreter: Sometimes the doctor writes a letter on a person. If the doctor writes a letter on you, you need further medical examinations.

Narrator: Although the family is scared, they walk past the doctor. He does not write on them.

Interpreter: Next, officials will ask you questions about your name, job, and the amount of money you have. I will help you answer. You need at least $18. How much do you have?

Father: I have $26. I have a skill. I was a baker in Europe.

Interpreter: I will tell the official.

Narrator: Soon the family finishes talking to the official. He nods, and the family is taken to the Money Exchange. There cashiers exchange American dollars for the money the immigrants carry.

Mother: At last we are done! Let's go to the Kissing Post.

Girl: What's the Kissing Post?

Mother: It's a wooden post where we meet your uncle and aunt.

Narrator: The family will live with relatives in a one-bedroom apartment in Manhattan. There will be nine people packed into a three-room apartment.

Boy: Finally! We are here in America!

Celebrating Culture

Objectives

- Read and talk to family members to learn more about personal culture.
- Identify specific elements unique to culture, such as food, dress, and celebrations.
- Identify similarities across cultures.
- Discuss ways cultures have blended to form American culture.

Quest Project-Based Learning: Create a Scrapbook

	Description	Duration	Materials	Participants
STEP 1 Set the Stage	Read a blackline master as an introduction to the Quest.	5 minutes	**Blackline Master:** Quest Kick Off	Whole Class
STEP 2 Launch the Activities				
Activity 1 Learning About My Culture	Read about cultures in a community; conduct a family interview to learn more about culture.	20 minutes	**Blackline Master:** Learning About My Culture **Graphic Organizer:** T-Chart **Content Reader:** The 10 Most Amazing Community Celebrations in the U.S.	Individuals
Activity 2 My Family Name	Create a family crest.	20 minutes	**Blackline Masters:** My Family Name; Learning About My Culture (completed) art supplies	Individuals
Activity 3 How My Culture Celebrates	Write a summary to explain a cultural celebration.	20 minutes	**Blackline Master:** Learning About My Culture (completed) **Graphic Organizer:** T-Chart art supplies	Individuals
Activity 4 America's Melting Pot	Interview a classmate to learn more about culture and how cultures work together to create an American culture.	30 minutes	**Blackline Masters:** America's Melting Pot; Learning About My Culture (completed) **Graphic Organizer:** T-Chart (partially completed)	Small Groups
STEP 3 Complete the Quest Create a Cultural Scrapbook	Create a cover and compile activity pages to create a cultural scrapbook.	10 minutes	**Blackline Masters:** My Family Name (completed); America's Melting Pot (completed) family celebration summary (completed), stapler, art supplies	Individuals
Deliver a **ELL** Presentation	Present cultural scrapbooks to the class.	30 minutes	Completed cultural scrapbooks	Individuals
Answer the **Compelling Question**	Discuss the answer to the compelling question.	10 minutes		Whole Class

Quick Activities

	Description	Duration	Materials	Participants
The History of Food	Read a fact sheet to learn about the history of "American" dishes.	15 minutes	**Blackline Master:** The History of Food **Student Activity Mat** 3B Time and Place	Individuals
Compare ELL **Celebrations**	Listen to a story and compare the celebration of an event in your own culture to the celebration of the same event in another culture.	20 minutes	**Graphic Organizer:** Venn Diagram *Throw Your Tooth on the Roof* by Selby Beeler	Small Groups
Uniquely American	Write an acrostic poem listing things that make you uniquely American.	20 minutes	timer	Individuals
Readers Theater: A Visit to the Cultural Fair	Perform a brief skit about visiting a cultural fair.	20 minutes	**Blackline Master:** A Visit to the Cultural Fair	Small Groups

Project-Based Learning: Celebrating Culture

Qompelling **Question** ## What is special about my culture?

Welcome to Quest 7, Celebrating Culture. In this Quest, students will investigate the things that make cultures unique and how these cultures have blended to become American culture. After participating in the Quest activities, students will be prepared to discuss the compelling question at the end of this inquiry.

Objectives

- Read and talk to family members to learn more about personal culture.
- Identify specific elements unique to culture, such as food, dress, and celebrations.
- Identify similarities across cultures.
- Discuss ways cultures have blended to form American culture.

STEP 1 Set the Stage ⏱ 5 minutes

Begin the Quest by distributing the blackline master, **Quest Kick Off.** It will bring the world of the Quest to life, introducing a story to interest students and a mission to motivate them.

Story

This Quest takes your students through a process of learning about their own culture while also being introduced to the cultures of their classmates. In doing so, they begin to identify things they share and develop an understanding of America's melting pot of culture.

· ·

Mission

Students are asked to create scrapbooks that tell about their family's culture to display at their school's Family Night event.

STEP 2 Launch the Activities

The following four activities will help students prepare their scrapbooks by helping them identify the things that make their culture special. Note that all four can be done independently of the larger Quest.

Activity 1 Learning About My Culture minutes

Materials: Blackline Master: Learning About My Culture, Graphic Organizer: T-Chart, Content Reader: The 10 Most Amazing Celebrations in the U.S.

Distribute the content reader, and have students read independently in order to learn more about cultural groups within a community. As students read, have them make notes on the graphic organizer **T-Chart.** On the left side of the chart, have students write the names of foods, dress, celebrations, or festivals that they have heard of, tried, or experienced. On the right side of the chart, have students list unfamiliar things.

Next, tell students to think about what they know about their own specific cultural group. Distribute the blackline master **Learning About My Culture,** which provides questions for students to answer about their own cultural group.

Instruct students to write the answers to questions they know on the page. Then have students take the blackline master home to review with family members who can give them additional details about their culture. Instruct students to bring the blackline master back to school for use in future activities.

Activity 2   My Family Name   (20) minutes

Materials: Blackline Master: My Family Name, Blackline Master: Learning About My Culture (completed), art supplies

Tell students that a family crest is a visual depiction of a family's history. Explain that family crests are used to give information about a family in pictures.

Distribute the blackline master **My Family Name,** which has a family crest to be completed in the activity.

Have students use the information from the blackline master **Learning About My Culture** to complete the sections of the family crest. In the top left square, have students write the word "Hello" in both English and the language of their cultural group. In the top right square, have students draw and label a picture of their family. In the bottom left square, have students draw and label a cultural food or traditional dish of their cultural group. In the bottom right square, have students draw and label an example of cultural dress. At the bottom of the crest, have students write their names and the name of their cultural group.

Note: Students who are part of a multicultural family should be encouraged to complete the activity in the way that they feel best honors their family's culture. This may be by combining the cultures in one crest, or it may be by creating two separate crests to show defining factors of the two cultures.

At the end of the activity, collect the blackline masters and set them aside to be used as the first page of the scrapbook.

Activity 3   How My Culture Celebrates   (20) minutes

Materials: Blackline Master: Learning About My Culture (completed), Graphic Organizer: T-Chart, art supplies

Have students return to their completed blackline master **Learning About My Culture** to remind themselves of cultural celebrations in which their families participate.

Distribute the graphic organizer **T-Chart,** which gives students space to make notes about their family celebrations. Tell students that in today's activity they will only be using the left side of the T-Chart. Instruct students to write the name of their family's cultural celebration on the left side of the T-Chart. Then have students write to answer the following questions about their family celebrations:

- When does it happen?
- Who comes together to celebrate?
- What types of things do you do?
- Why does your family participate in this celebration?

To culminate, instruct students to write a brief summary that explains the celebration to others, answering the questions when, who, what, and why.

Collect the T-Charts to be used in a later activity. Collect the summaries to be used as the second page of the scrapbook.

Activity 4 **America's Melting Pot** minutes

Materials: Blackline Masters: America's Melting Pot; Learning About My Culture (completed); Graphic Organizer: T-Chart (partially completed)

Divide students into mixed cultural groups and have students discuss the celebrations they enjoy with their families. Distribute the graphic organizer **T-Chart** and instruct students to choose a partner of a different culture to continue the activity. Have students label the right side of the T-Chart with the name of the other student's cultural group. Then have the student ask and write the answers to the when, who, what, and why questions as used in the previous activity. After the partners have finished their discussions, have students analyze their notes to look for similarities in their different cultural celebrations.

Distribute the blackline master **America's Melting Pot,** which gives students space to highlight the similarities between their culture and their partner's culture. Instruct students to draw an illustration of their own celebration on the left and label the name of their own culture. On the right, have students draw an illustration of the partner's celebration and label the name of the partner's culture. At the bottom, have the students write to explain the similarities between the two cultures.

To culminate, have students return to the completed blackline master **Learning About My Culture.** Instruct students to refer to the final entry on the page (American traditions that my family enjoys that have come from a different culture). Explain to students that America has become known as a melting pot of cultures. Explain that many of us living in America enjoy celebrating the diverse cultures of the groups who live here. Allow student volunteers to name American traditions or celebrations that their families participate in that have come from another culture. Explain that having the freedom to experience so many different cultures is one of the many wonderful things about being an American.

Collect the blackline masters to be used as the third page in the scrapbook.

STEP 3 Complete the

Part 1 **Create a Cultural Scrapbook** (10) minutes

Materials: Blackline Masters: My Family Name, America's Melting Pot (completed); family celebration summary (completed), stapler, art supplies

Have students combine the pages completed during the Quest activities to make a scrapbook. First, have students create a cover for the scrapbook. Encourage students to use colors that are important to their culture and to use this space to draw illustrations that relate to their culture. Then have students place the scrapbook pages in order as they were completed during the Quest activities: **My Family Name,** the summary of the family celebration, and **America's Melting Pot.**

Part 2 **Deliver a Presentation** minutes

Have students deliver a presentation in which they present their scrapbooks to the class. If possible, invite parents to attend the scrapbook presentations. Have each student come to the front of the classroom and share each page of his or her scrapbook, explaining what makes his or her culture special and identifying how the culture has influenced American dress, foods, and celebrations.

· ·

ⓔⓛⓛ Support for English Language Learners

Speaking Explain to students that speaking clearly helps listeners to better understand the ideas that are being presented.

Entering: Prior to presenting the scrapbook, allow the student time to practice one on one. Point to one image on a page of the scrapbook that relates to the student's culture and say the name of the image aloud. Have the student repeat the English word after you. Continue practice until the student is confident enough to present his or her scrapbook to a small group while saying the word.

Emerging: Prior to presenting the scrapbook, allow the student time to practice one on one. Point to one image on a page of the scrapbook that relates to the student's culture and state a sentence related to that image aloud. Have the student repeat the sentence after you. Continue practice until the student is confident enough to present his or her scrapbook to a small group while saying the sentence.

Developing: Prior to presenting the scrapbook, allow the student time to practice with a partner. Have the partners practice saying sentences relating to each of the three pages. Have the partners continue practice with saying the three sentences aloud until they are confident enough to present their scrapbooks to a small group while saying the sentences.

Expanding: Prior to presenting the scrapbook, allow the student time to practice with a small group. Have the student practice saying one to two sentences relating to each of the three pages, and have the group respond to the presentation with feedback. Have the student continue practicing until he or she is confident enough to present the scrapbook to the class.

Bridging: Prior to presenting the scrapbook, allow the student time to practice with a small group. Have the student practice giving the presentation to the group, and have the group respond to the presentation with feedback. Have the student continue practicing until he or she is confident enough to present the scrapbook to the class.

Part 3 **Answer the Compelling Question** minutes

After students finish presenting their scrapbooks, encourage them to reflect on what they learned. As a class, discuss the compelling question for this Quest "What is special about my culture?"

Students have learned the special things about their own personal cultures and how different cultures have blended to become American culture. They should use what they learned to answer the compelling question.

Quest Kick Off

Celebrating Culture

Your principal wants to host a Family Night event at your school but needs your help! Your principal needs a display for the event that will showcase the diversity of the students who attend your school. At the Family Night event, your principal wants the families who attend to be able to learn about the cultural groups represented by the students. Your principal has asked for your help in creating a display that will help introduce families to different cultures.

Your Mission

Create scrapbooks that tell the story of your family's culture. In your scrapbook, use words and pictures to help teach others about the things that make your culture special. As you work to create your scrapbook, think about the special things you see in your classmates' cultures and how all of these cultures come together to make us Americans.

To create your scrapbook:

Activity 1 **Learning About My Culture:** Read to learn about different cultures in a community, then interview your family to learn more about your culture.

Activity 2 **My Family Name:** Create a family crest to show the special things about your family's culture.

Activity 3 **How My Culture Celebrates:** Investigate and illustrate a cultural celebration.

Activity 4 **America's Melting Pot:** Interview a classmate to learn more about his or her culture and how your cultures work together to create an American culture.

Complete Your Quest

Use your completed activities to create and present a cultural scrapbook.

Name _____ Date _____

Learning About My Culture

Think about what you already know about your cultural group. Fill in the answers you already know. At home, interview family members to learn more about your culture and answer any unanswered questions. Bring this sheet back to school to use in the Quest.

My cultural group:

_____

Traditional foods my family enjoys:

_____

_____

Dress of my culture:

_____

How people say "hello" in my culture's language:

_____

Ways that people in my culture have fun:

_____

_____

American traditions that my family enjoys that have come from a different culture:

_____

_____

_____

My Family Name

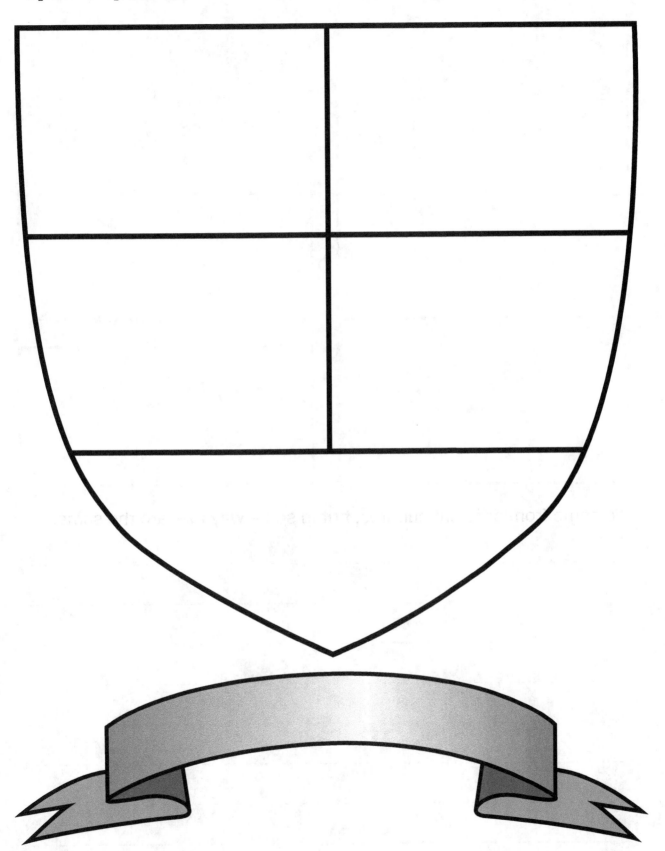

Name _____ Date _____

America's Melting Pot

We come from different cultures, but in some ways we are the same.

_____

_____

_____

_____

_____

_____

_____

The History of Food

Individuals (15) minutes

Materials: Blackline Master: The History of Food, Student Activity Mat 3B
Time and Place

Explain to students that foods such as pizza, hot dogs, tacos, and even sandwiches have their origins in other countries but are now well-known foods to American people. Provide a brief explanation to students to provide background information on how these foods came to be known as American staples.

America has often been called a melting pot of cultures. This is because immigrants from all over the world have traveled here to make America their home. When they came, they brought their favorite things with them, including their treasured family recipes. Once in America, these families continued to make the foods they had loved to eat. Pretty soon, other people tried these foods and discovered that they were delicious! So many people began eating these cultural foods that they "melted" into American culture. Now in America we enjoy foods from all over the world.

Distribute the blackline master **The History of Food,** which provides the history of four "American" dishes: pizza, hot dogs, tacos, and sandwiches.

As students read the blackline master, have them use Student Activity Mat 3B Time and Place to trace the path from the food's country of origin to its place of introduction in the United States. Then, have students fold a sheet of paper into quadrant squares. Tell students to draw and label each of the foods and to include the food's country of origin.

Compare Celebrations

Materials: Graphic Organizer: Venn Diagram, *Throw Your Tooth on the Roof* by Selby Beeler

Tell students that something all families share is the desire to celebrate together. Explain that families of different backgrounds often celebrate the same holidays or events in different ways.

Distribute the graphic organizer **Venn Diagram.** Tell students you will read a book about the ways different families celebrate a lost tooth. Before beginning the story, organize students into small groups and assign each child a country. Tell students that as you read their assigned country's section, they should make notes on the back of the graphic organizer about how the country celebrates the event.

Read aloud the book *Throw Your Tooth on the Roof* by Selby Beeler, pausing after each section. During the pauses, allow groups to discuss the section and allow time for groups to make notes about their assigned countries. When the book is finished, tell groups to work together to complete their Venn diagrams to compare and contrast ways that this event is celebrated in their own homes.

Support for English Language Learners

Writing Explain to students that comparing is when we look for things that are alike and contrasting is when we look for things that are different.

Entering: Have students draw and label one way that this event is celebrated in their homes.

Emerging: Have students draw and label one way that this event is celebrated in their homes. Then turn to a page in the book and have students draw and label how the event is celebrated in the student's home in the book. Explain that this is comparing the two events to show how they are alike.

Developing: Have students write to tell how the event is celebrated in their homes. Then turn to a page in the book and ask students to name how the celebration in the book is the same as their celebration and how it is different.

Expanding: Have students write on the left side of the Venn diagram to tell how the event is celebrated in their homes. Then turn to a page in the book and have students identify similarities between their celebration and the celebration of the student in the book. Have students cross out similarities written on the left side of the graphic organizer and write them in the center.

Bridging: Have students write on the left side of the Venn diagram to tell how the event is celebrated in their homes. Then turn to a page in the book and have students identify similarities between their celebration and the celebration of the student in the book. Have students cross out similarities written on the left side of the graphic organizer and write them in the center. Then have students identify differences between the two celebrations and write these on the right side of the Venn diagram.

Uniquely American

Materials: timer

Set a timer for 5 minutes and instruct students to write down all the things that come to mind when they hear the word *American.* When time has elapsed, allow students to read the things from their lists as you write them on the board. (Students should respond with things such as baseball, apple pie, Fourth of July, football, or Thanksgiving.)

Next, tell students to write the name of their culture at the top of a sheet of paper. Set a timer for 5 minutes and instruct students to write down all the things that come to mind when they think of their specific cultural group. When time has elapsed, allow students to read the things from their lists as you write them on the board.

Ask students to think about what makes them American.

Ask: *Do the things on your cultural list keep you from being an American?* (no)

Explain that bringing different aspects of culture to America is what makes all of us Americans. We are all a part of a uniquely American culture.

Have students write an acrostic poem using the letters in their first name. Tell students that for each letter, they should list something that makes them uniquely American. For example:

S-wedish roots
A-merican born
R-aring to play softball
A-lways in the mood for pizza

At the bottom of the poem, instruct students to write the sentence: I am uniquely American.

The History of Food

The History of Pizza

Pizza was first eaten in Naples, a city in Italy. Workers in the city of Naples needed something that could be made quickly, tasted great, and could be eaten using only their hands. Pizza was perfect!

These delicious slices stayed tucked away in Naples until the first immigrants began to arrive in New York, bringing their recipes for the spicy pies with them. These workers were coming to America looking for factory work, not trying to bring a new dish, but that is just what happened! Before long other Americans were asking for a taste, and soon, people of all cultures could be seen with a slice.

Today, both New York and Chicago are well known for their distinctive style of pizzas.

The History of Hot Dogs

It is widely believed that the hot dog (or frankfurter, as it was originally called) was created in Frankfurt, Germany, in 1487. While the reports on who actually sold the first hot dog in America are debated, we know that hot dogs were frequently sold on street carts in major American cities by immigrants who had traveled to live in America.

In 1893, large groups of visitors in Chicago, Illinois, tried these handy little meals. They enjoyed the toppings, such as sauerkraut, and loved that they were able to be eaten with just one hand.

The hot dog—quick, easy, and inexpensive—quickly caught on at American baseball games and could soon be seen nestled in the hands of hungry Americans everywhere.

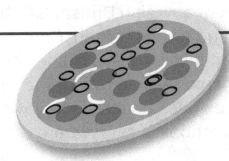

The History of Tacos

As a staple of Mexican (and now American) dinners, tacos have surprisingly little known about their history. Maybe early Mexicans believed a food this tasty could speak for itself!

It is widely believed that tacos got their start in the silver mines of Mexico. The first type of taco to be named was the *taco de minero,* which translates to "the miner's taco." It was a tightly rolled, meat-filled tortilla, looking more like a taquito than the tacos we know today. If you look at a taquito, you will see its resemblance to a stick of miner's dynamite.

Tacos were first spotted in America in Los Angeles in the 1900s, brought by Mexican migrant workers. However, it was not until the birth of a popular food chain restaurant, Taco Bell, that many Americans were introduced to this spicy Mexican treat. Today, tacos are enjoyed by people all over America.

The History of Sandwiches

The sandwich as we know it today has been attributed to John Montagu, fourth Earl of Sandwich. John Montagu, a resident of England who loved playing cards, was deep into an exciting card game. He called for his cook and asked the cook to prepare a meal for him that he could eat while continuing to play. The cook returned with slices of roast beef between two pieces of toast, and the sandwich was born.

Of course, that is only one story. Other historians believe that Montagu saw similar foods being eaten by people in Greece and Turkey and simply copied their idea. What is known is that Montagu made the sandwich popular among the wealthy people in England.

The sandwich is not mentioned in America until its appearance in an 1816 cookbook. The colonists, eager to separate themselves from anything British, left their sandwiches behind. Once America was established and their memories had faded, the sandwich was back, much to the joy of lunchboxes everywhere.

Readers Theater
A Visit to the Cultural Fair

In this Readers Theater, you will act as a family visiting the park to enjoy a community's cultural fair.

The Parts

4 players:

- **Mom**
- **Dad**
- **Child**
- **Tour Guide**

Director's Notes:

Mom, Dad, and Child enter from stage right. They walk toward Tour Guide, who is standing stage left.

Child:	I'm so excited to visit the cultural fair today!
Mom:	I am, too. I think we will learn lots of new things about the people who live in our community.
Dad:	I wonder how we should begin.
Child:	There's a tour guide, Dad. Let's ask.

pointing at Tour Guide

Mom, Dad, and Child approach Tour Guide, who is looking down at hands as though studying a map of the park.

Mom:	Excuse me?

Tour Guide looks up, then smiles at Mom, Dad, and Child.

Tour Guide:	Well, hello! Welcome to our community cultural fair.
Mom:	Thank you. We're wondering where we should begin. Can you help?

Tour Guide:
turns to the side and points

I can help you with that! At the left side of the park we've set up our cultural games section. We have games from all over the world along with members of our community who can teach you how to play.

Child:
jumping with excitement

Oh boy, that sounds like fun!

Tour Guide:

At the right of the park we have our "Eat Around the World" section, where you can try foods from many different nations.

Dad:
looks at Child and smiles

Mmmm, I hope they have Italian ice!

Child:

Yummy! And baklava!

Mom:

Oh, yes, I love that Turkish dessert! And maybe they'll even have some American apple pie, too!

Tour Guide:

Man, you guys are making me hungry!

All players laugh.

Tour Guide:

In the center of the park, we have a schedule of cultural dances. Some of them even let the audience participate.

Mom:

Oh, dancing! I hope they have some American Indian dances. They are so wonderful to see.

Child:

I'm ready to see everything!

Tour Guide:

Enjoy your trip around the world!

Tour Guide and family wave goodbye as family walks past to exit stage.

K-W-L Chart

What We **K**now	What We **W**ant to Know	What We **L**earned

Web

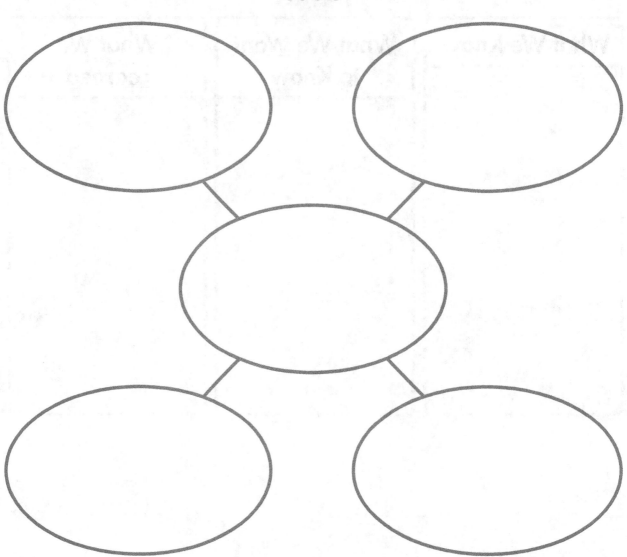

Main Idea and Details

Main Idea

Supporting Detail	Supporting Detail	Supporting Detail

Venn Diagram

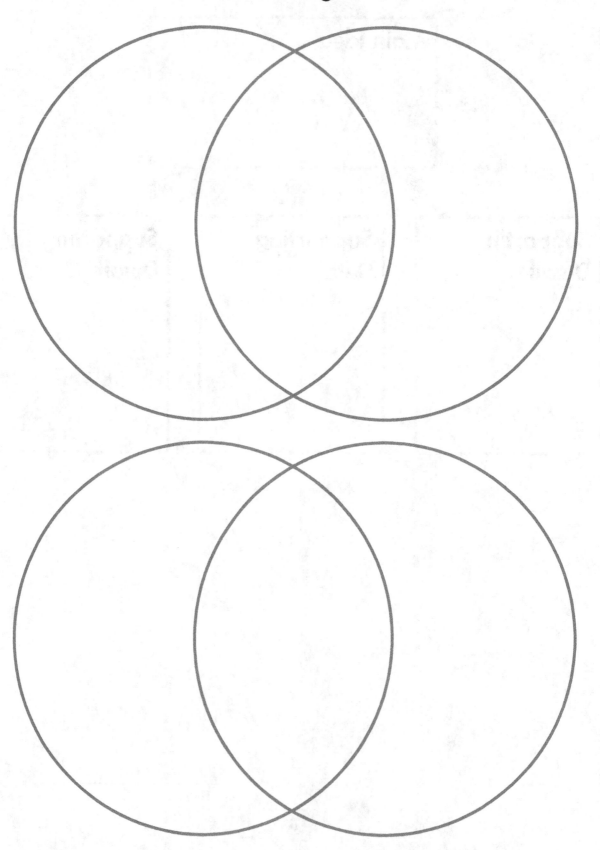

Compare and Contrast

Topics

Alike

Different

Cause and Effect

Causes

Effects

Why did it happen?	→	**What happened?**
Why did it happen?	→	**What happened?**
Why did it happen?	→	**What happened?**

Problem and Solution A

Problem

Solution

Problem and Solution B

Problem

How I Tried to Solve the Problem

Solution

Steps in a Process A

Process

....

....

Step 1

↓

Step 2

Step 3

Steps in a Process B

Process

....

....

Step 1

Step 2

Step 3

Step 4

T-Chart

Three-Column Chart

Four-Column Chart

Outline Form

Title

....

....

A. ....

    1. ....

    2. ....

    3. ....

B. ....

    1. ....

    2. ....

    3. ....

C. ....

    1. ....

    2. ....

    3. ....

Answer Key

Chapter 1

Quest Activity 2: The Five Regions of the United States, p. 9

1. the Southwest
2. the Southeast
3. the Southeast
4. the Southwest
5. the Northeast
6. the Midwest and Southeast
7. the West

Chapter 2

Quick Activity: Business Model, p. 30

The resources listed should make sense for the business students choose.

Chapter 3

Quest Activity 1: Quartering Act, p. 43

(Possible answers:)

Who: British rule forced on American colonists
What: forced colonists to provide food, supplies, and housing to British soldiers stationed in the colonies
When: 1765
Where: American colonies
Why: to ensure colonists were obeying British laws and paying British taxes

Quest Activity 2: Stamp Act, p. 44

(Possible answers:)

Who: British rule forced on American colonists
What: forced colonists to pay a tax on all paper goods
When: 1765
Where: American colonies
Why: to help Britain gain money from the colonists' need to access information

Quest Activity 2: Townshend Acts, p. 45

(Possible answers:)

Who: British rule forced on American colonists
What: forced colonists to pay a tax on goods imported from Britain
When: 1767
Where: American colonies
Why: to gain more money from the colonists through taxation

Quest Activity 3: The Colonists Strike Back, p. 46

(Possible answers:)

Who: American colonists
What: a protest in which the colonists dumped tea into Boston Harbor
When: 1773
Where: Boston Harbor
Why: to make a statement to Britain that the colonists were unhappy with the unfair taxation and rules of the British.

Quest Activity 3: The Coercive Acts, p. 47
(Possible answers:)
Who: British Parliament
What: passed a series of acts known as the Coercive Acts
When: 1774
Where: American colonies
Why: to punish the colonists for the Boston Tea Party

Quick Activity 1: Match the Act, p. 52
Students should complete the table as follows:

Coercive Acts	A series of acts passed by British Parliament in order to punish the colonists for the Boston Tea Party.
Quartering Act	Forced colonists to provide food, housing, and supplies to British soldiers stationed in the colonies.
First Continental Congress	Assembly in which colonists agreed to begin working toward independence for America.
Stamp Act	Placed new taxes on paper goods in the colonies.
Townshend Acts	Placed increased taxes on goods which were imported from Britain.
Boston Tea Party	Protest led by colonists in which 342 chests of tea were thrown into Boston Harbor.

Chapter 4

No answers required for this chapter.

Chapter 5

No answers required for this chapter.

Chapter 6

No answers required for this chapter.

Chapter 7

No answers required for this chapter.

Image Credits

Chapter 01
016: Jon Bilous/Shutterstock

Chapter 05
091T: Anthony Berger/Library of Congress Prints and Photographs Division [LC-DIG-ppmsca-19305]; 091C: North Wind Picture Archives/Alamy Stock Photo; 091B: Georgios Kollidas/Shutterstock; 092T: Maxfocus/E+/Getty Images; 092TC: Glasshouse Images/JT Vintage/Alamy Stock Photo; 092B: Bettmann/Getty Images; 092BC: National Archives/Stocktrek Images/Getty Images; 097B: Nsf/Alamy Stock Photo

Chapter 06
121: Jan Walters/Alamy Stock Photo; 123: Myles Santiago/Shutterstock